*T. Walker Dee*

# Prodigal Father Waiting Son

## One man's lifelong journey to forgive his father.

Prodigal Father, Waiting Son


Version 2, 2nd Edition

ISBN: 978-0-557-14886-8

Published by Ridgeway Publications
11607 Ridgeway Ct., Holland, MI  49424



This is a work of non-fiction however the author has changed the names of people in order to protect their privacy and anonymity.

# Contents

# ~ To My Kids ~

Our church has been very gracious and has granted me a sabbatical leave. I am neither burning out nor growing frustrated with ministry, quite the contrary. There have been no restrictions given to my three months away from church responsibilities. I can fish, sleep, go to soccer games and hang out with all of you and no one would think twice about it. However, I am spending many beautiful May, June and July days in the Seminary library typing on my laptop because I want you to know. I want you to know my wounds, the healing that comes from God, and the power of forgiveness. I want you to, one day, understand the things about me that came up short, but also understand the things that have been so painful to me have motivated me to instruct you, to build your character in such ways that you never do to another what has been done to me. Claire and Scott, know that I love you more than life itself. Understand why I want you to never treat things like they are more important than people. Know why truth is always important. See why I want you to be respectful of your mom. Also for me, please understand that every time I miss an event, raise my voice, or end up going to a meeting instead of being with you, I get "the guilts"because I fear you may one day see me the same way I have seen my dad.

He's not a bad man. He just doesn't really know how to love. He never did any of these things to hurt me or wound me. He just did what was easy instead of what was right. Now, hopefully, you will understand better what makes me tick and why doing right instead of doing what is easy is so important to me.

Dad

# ~ Intro ~

As you begin reading this story, this journey of forgiveness, I (the author) ask you to keep three things in mind:

1) The end of the story is where I live, how I think, and what I believe is a healthier way to experience life. Because I have been blessed with a decent memory and am a person who is self-aware, I have recounted each event and story with the memories (both emotional and chronological) in a way that expresses how I *felt* at the time. In other words, I attempted to "tell on myself" with the hope that you (the reader) would find yourself in the story, recognize your own responses, reactions, and, sometimes, unproductive assumptions.

Memories are tricky. I have no doubt other members of my family, including my dad, have different takes on the same events. However, the events recounted in this book are my memories. There has been no attempt to dramatize, tweak or change what I remember.

2) This book is not intended to be a scholarly work. It is simply one very large part of my story. It is often raw, always honest and does not attempt to paint a positive self portrait. These experiences were difficult, painful and injurious, though no more so (and often less so) than yours.

This book was written for my kids because they have witnessed bits and pieces of my journey over the years and I wanted them to have an opportunity to learn from my mistakes and from some of the wisdom I have gleaned over the years.

3) While this is a work of non-fiction, I have changed the names of each person in the story (including my own) because it is not about the people as much as about the lessons learned.

## *Chapter 1*

# "As I Remember It"

### *~ Betrayal ~*

My mom had been crying off and on over the last several days. I noticed she had been looking at the newspaper a lot. I had heard nothing about a war, a natural disaster or economic problems. Then again, I was eleven years old, the internet was not yet invented, there was no such thing as a personal computer, and whenever the President came on television, I went upstairs to my room.

That Saturday evening, my mom and dad were downstairs. My brothers and I were in our room and we were talking…wondering what was going on with Mom. Soon, I found myself 'elected' to go downstairs and find out. While I wasn't the oldest child in the family of six (Mom, Dad, three brothers and me), I did play that role.

I walked down the stairs, eased into the family room, and again, saw my mom looking at the paper…the want ads. My dad was there, they were both teary. I asked, "What's wrong?" They looked at each other, paused, and my dad proceeded to tell me he was leaving. He traveled a lot for work, so it took me a moment to understand. He was LEAVING. I got the whole speech parents give when their marriage isn't going to make it: "It's not your fault. Sometimes mommies and daddies just drift apart. I'm not leaving you boys. I still love your mom. It's just not working." Etc.

As I was leaving the family room, trying to ready my 'report' for my brothers, my dad told me not to "tell the boys." He said it should come from him.

"When will you tell 'em?' I asked

"We're going to have one more weekend as a family. We're going to go skiing together on Sunday. I'll tell them after that," my father said.

That was the day my "dad" became my "father." That was the day he betrayed me. That was the day he began the divorce proceedings. I was angry, hurt, betrayed, humiliated and would not trust another thing he told me for almost thirty years. He was not only divorcing my mom, he was leaving me, divorcing me and betraying me. Please don't read this wrong. These were not the thoughts of my father; they were mine. *How could he ask me to keep this secret? How could he leave, after all the talk about carrying on our family's good name? How could he do this to my mom?*

I went upstairs, walked past the room where my brothers were waiting, and in to my own. As I lay on the bed, it occurred to me that I should be sad…I should cry. I was numb.

Sunday came and we skied. I skied hard. I looked no one in the eye, said little and waited for the trip home--for the moment when I heard the news again…the speech again. I waited to experience the moment when my brothers realized they were betrayed; by my father and by me. I knew. They would know I knew.

Monday morning, he left. God I loved him. Oh, how I hated him. *Leave you jerk. Please turn around and say you are sorry, try again. Get out of hear you SOB.* I would never be the same.

## *~ Visits ~*

Remembering the next two years is difficult. Not because it hurts, but because I was a pre-teen trying to figure out how to be the 'man of the house' and trying to control the changes in my body, my new school and the social structure among peers.

I recall my father visiting on occasion. He would rent a hotel room, swing by the house and pick one or all of us up, take us to the hotel, buy us all the candy and pop we wanted, let us swim in the pool, stay up too late, and then take us home the next day. I went because I was supposed to. I went because my mother said I should. And each time I enjoyed myself, I felt guilty for loving my father when my mother was home alone. When I returned, I felt guilty for hating my father the way I did and always wondered how this could be.

Sitting in a parking lot across the street from our house, as my father was dropping me off, he asked me, "So…..is your mother dating? Is she seeing anyone?"

Astonished and surprised, I said, "No.....you?"

"Yea. You know, I have to move on. It's what you have to do."

*What? It's what you have to do? This is what you wanted to talk about in the parking lot of my middle school across the street from my home...our home?*

As I walked across the street, I wished I had had the guts to ask the questions. Instead, I retreated to the home of my new friends: anger, betrayal and self-absorption.

## ~ *Are you Melinda?* ~

My brothers and I learned to work the system. Double birthdays, double Christmases, etc. My father was doing well for himself, and each year after he left, would give the boys a membership (season passes) at our local ski resort. In one of the few civil conversations I remember between my mom and father, she asked if she could 'join' the family plan for the season passes in order to save money over an individual membership. He agreed, as long as she paid the difference.

Late in the fall, my mom, brothers and I went to the office of the ski resort to get our photos taken for our season pass. After each photo was taken, the customer service rep. would ask our name, birth date and city of residence. When my mom's picture was taken, the woman asked, "Are you Melinda?" My mom's name is Francis. My mom stumbled, stuttered, regained her composure and said, "No, I'm Francis." The costumer service rep. asked, "Then who is Melinda?"

This is how we found out. This is how we got the news. This....this was the announcement....my father was married! I had never met her, never heard of her. They had been married the weekend after the divorce was final. On the way home, we got additional news. My older brother, Alex, had been at the wedding.

I am sure my father had considered all the options: wondered if we should know, debated inviting us to the wedding, weighed the pros and cons, considered our feelings, and made what he thought was the best and right choice. However, we should have heard the news from him.

He was gone. As it turned out, he had been gone for years. The relationship with Melinda (Mindy) was the primary reason for my parents' divorce. They had been having an ongoing affair for seven years prior to the separation. He had chosen Mindy over us.

## *~ Rent Free ~*

Remember I was two weeks away from being twelve years old when my father left. From the day he left to the day he was re-married, just over two years had passed. I do not claim my thinking or memories are either righteous or one hundred percent accurate, but my memories are mine, and the way I processed the experiences and information during that time changed me…forever.

As with most early adolescents, my world was pretty small. I assumed everyone knew my shortcomings, noticed my clumsiness and would all point at the huge zit I had on my nose as I walked the halls of my middle school. I was obsessed with girls, always trying to impress the cool guys and was willing to do almost anything to be received, befriended and accepted by anyone I considered worth my adoration.

What others didn't know was that my father was living rent free in my head most of the time. I was conflicted…always. I loved him dearly. I wanted him to call me and apologize for what he had done to me. Desperately I craved a call from him inviting me to a father/son outing or event. However, I knew I would resent it if he asked, turn him down and maybe, just maybe have the guts to tell him off.

Most of my self-image revolved around masking the fact that I was the abandoned little boy. I dove into sports, and created a self confident, even cocky demeanor. I vowed I would never be disloyal; would never betray a friend or my family. I fantasized about my parents getting back together, while at the same time wanting my father to suffer; I hoped for his new marriage to end while trying to earn his approval by getting to know Mindy. I wanted him to be my "dad" again but knew I would never let him be any more than my "father."

In other words, he controlled much of the way I thought, acted, behaved and believed, though he had no idea. He was living in my head, controlling my psyche, remodeling my personality, all the while believing he was doing a pretty good job of fathering his boys in the midst of a broken family.

I vowed I would never forgive him.

## *Chapter 2*

# "Breaking My Vow"

### *~ Sophomore (wise fool) ~*

Immediately following the separation, my father moved to Mississippi. After a year, he moved to Detroit. My freshman year, he and Mindy moved to the west side of the state, one mile from our home.

He tried to invest himself in our lives. He showed up to a few games, volunteered to assist in coaching and was even recognized in the local (very local) paper as "volunteer of the month." I resented him playing dad, while making me and my mother miserable. My brothers had different 'stuff', carried different baggage and decided to react and respond differently than I. Alex would have done anything for my father's approval but always felt he missed the mark. Randy went overboard with girls and booze and played the game between mom and father better than any of us. Trip, the youngest, didn't know any different. He was in kindergarten when my father left, so his memories our broken family included no recollection of a family in tact.

After my freshman year, I went to a Young Life camp outside of Buena Vista, CO. I learned I was loved by another Father who would never let me down, never betray me and would always be there when I needed him. I gave my life to Christ.

I poured myself in to my new found faith. I had friends who knew me and my story. I had adult men who invested in me and I had purpose. I would live for God.

I studied. I learned. I memorized Scripture verses. I went to Bible studies, gave my testimony at the Rotary Club, treated people better, listened to other kids who were hurting, and shared my faith when I could. In short, I thought 2 Corinthians 5:17 had been made manifest in me. "Therefore, if anyone is in Christ, he is a new creation; the old has gone, the new has come! (NIV)"

Naively, I hoped and believed that I was done with the anger, betrayal and hurt that had driven me for so long. The mask of 'having it all together', of being confident was no longer a mask. I had found what I was looking for and would be fine from this point forward. Don't read me wrong. I wholeheartedly believe God can and often does deliver people from much greater bondage than mine. He would have and could have delivered me from mine in one fell swoop, but He didn't. However, I took one mask off and replaced it with another. I was now free from my father and devoted to my Father. This was my proclamation, but it was not my behavior.

After coming to Christ in 1981, a journey began. It was a road marked with signs and wonders, but also roadblocks, pot holes and speed bumps. As I grew in faith and devoted myself to discipleship, I used my story to help others. I spoke freely of the pain and betrayal I felt when my father left. I was willing to share with anyone who asked. Throughout high school I had many opportunities to speak in front of large groups of people.

While I was developing in faith, my father was starting and growing a new business. Things went well. He was one of the faithful fathers who paid child support and alimony. He complained, especially to me, but he paid. Over the course of those few years, I had become the family confidant and counselor. Both my mother and father shared things with me, believing I was trustworthy (which I was) and mature enough to handle it. Unbeknownst to them, I may have been wise beyond my years as far as my counsel was concerned, but I desperately wanted both of them to stop telling me things a kid shouldn't know. I offered, I listened and I never betrayed. But I wanted to be a kid, not a parent to my parents.

As my father's business grew, he made some decisions that created circumstances with which the bank became increasingly uncomfortable. They called in the loan; he didn't have the cash on hand. They froze his assets. Suddenly he was broke. Bankruptcy proceedings began. My father approached me soon after the hearing at the bank. He asked me to speak with my mother and ask her to give him a six month reprieve from his child support and alimony payments. Why he asked me, I don't know, but it seemed natural at the time. It seems kind of sick now, but that was our family system. So, at the insistence (framed in a request) of my father, I spoke with my mom to "broker a deal" for him until he could get his feet back on the ground. My mom agreed.

That was the last time he ever paid alimony or child support. Our livelihood was gone. Our standard of living went from running with the Jones' to avoiding calls from creditors. My mom's savings were depleted, her hope was leached and her spirit became increasingly bitter. All the while, my father continued to promise he would start the payments again as soon as he "got back on his feet." He never failed to share with me how hard it was on him, nor did he acknowledge how hard it was on us.

There is a silver lining in this gloomy cloud. Due to his bankruptcy and my grades, college would cost me next to nothing.

## *~ A God Moment ~*

Adolescent angst was the norm for me during my early and mid high school years. I was a new Christian with a conscience but struggled to make the lifestyle changes I believed the Lord wanted me to make. Like most kids, I struggled internally with whether or not I was cool, wondered if girls liked me (why and why not?) and I spent much of my alone time assuming everyone else was thinking about my hair or any zits I happened to have. I assumed as I walked the halls that many of the conversations whispered from one person to another were probably about me ... and they probably weren't whispering, "wow, he's so cool!"

I remember walking home from school several days in a row with an endless loop of Genesis' "Lonely Man on the Corner" and Phil Collins' "I Don't Care Anymore" on my off-brand Walkman®. For those of you reading this who were born in the 1980's or later, a Walkman® was my generation's iPod®, only with a cassette tape instead of a flash or hard drive. I was depressed. I was navigating life in a rut, which is just a grave with both ends kicked out. I had little or no joy. Though I faked it pretty well when in public, my internal life was full of sorrow, grief, anger and angst.

Honestly I don't remember if much or most of my depression was due to my father having left, the financial crunch my family found itself in, or simply a normal teen identity crisis. I do know one thing for certain, whatever the cause, I placed the blame for most of my problems on my father.

Spring Break my junior year of high school, I went to Florida (Disney World®, Sea World®, Cypress Gardens® and Daytona Beach) with a local youth group. In the group was an old girlfriend of mine, one of my best friends from my high school, and a bunch of people I only knew from the youth group. We road down on a bus and I teetered back and forth between engaging others, playing euchre and sitting alone looking out the window. One evening, having slept on a church floor by night and visiting various amusement parks by day, our group was eating pizza at a local restaurant in Winter Haven, FL. If memory serves me correctly, I took a self-righteous stance about a song playing on the juke box (I refuse to explain what a juke box is). My former girlfriend overheard my comment and took me to task. I don't recall exactly what she said but I knew two things: She was absolutely right, and I needed to get away from all these people for a while. I told the leader I was going back to the church and started walking the three or four blocks. Once on the church grounds, I sat in the front lawn.

I started talking to God out loud. I listed all the things wrong with my life as I saw them. It started with being angry at my former girlfriend and quickly moved to my issues with my dad. Fifteen or twenty minutes later I was out of words. On the lawn, my arms around my knees and head down, I said one last thing to God, "What is WRONG with me?" It wasn't loud but immediately after uttering those words I perceived someone approaching. I looked up and saw an "old guy" walking down the sidewalk. He was wearing sandals, very baggy and dirty pants and a hemp shirt from Mexico that was popular with hippy types back then. His hair was gray and very long. It was in a pony tail, bound by twine crisscrossed from the back of his head all the way down. I put my head back down and snickered. I don't remember my exact thought, but I'm sure 'geek' came to mind. I also hoped he hadn't overheard me.

As he neared me, ten or twenty feet away, he left the sidewalk and eased toward me. I looked up again and he asked, "You OK?"

As politely as I could muster I said, "Yup, just thinking."

In a very non-judgmental tone, this guy looked me dead in the eye and said, "No you're not. You're feeling sorry for yourself."

I smiled sarcastically, put my head down and thought, "who does this guy think he……HOLY CRAP!"

I looked up, seconds had passed…maybe five, seven tops and he was gone. I was in the middle of the block, there was no where he could have gone, but he was no where to be found. Gone. "Holy Crap," I whispered this time. God had just answered my prayer.

"What is WRONG with me?" God said, "You're feeling sorry for yourself."

I honestly don't know if this was an angelic visitation or not, though I have no other explanation. Regardless of the man's origins, earthly or heavenly, I knew God had spoken directly to me….through a man I had judged on appearance alone. God cared enough for me to tell me what was wrong. I adjusted my attitude for the rest of the week and resolved to no longer feel sorry for myself. I would deal with things directly, learn how others experienced me and make decisions about adjustments to my behavior based on the knowledge of others' perception of me weighed against who I believed God was creating me to be. If I decided to change, it would be because I believed God was teaching me through others, not because I wanted to be liked.

I adjusted my lifestyle to a standard I believed God was expecting and, while I had come to Christ a few years prior, I began to get to know Him in a very new and very real way. I was becoming a Christ follower, not just a believer. I grew in knowledge of Him; not just about Him. That experience in Winter Haven, FL was a critical one, though as I look back on it, I didn't learn as much from it as I believe God was trying to teach.

## ~ *Tasted blessing* ~

As I entered college, I began volunteering for Young Life as a leader in a few local Young Life Clubs. Through that involvement I was recognized as a leader and was chosen to give my testimony at a local revival at Calvin College called Alive '85. I told the story of

God's grace in my life to thousands. When I left the stage, the evangelist grabbed me and asked, "Have you considered big time evangelism as your calling?" I was ecstatic! While I had previously believed I was called to the ministry and knew God had his hand on my life, I was overwhelmingly encouraged that a man of this stature would confirm my calling in an offhand/side bar comment. My future was set. I would serve the Lord. There were some things I had to change, but I would follow God's path for me. I had been in a relationship with a young lady that had become sexual. I was living a double life. I had to get out of that relationship and devote myself to the service of my King. My girlfriend and I argued constantly. After half a dozen break-ups, the relationship was over.

Feeling responsible for my part in the loss of the family livelihood (brokering the deal for my father that he had no intention of honoring), I decided to make right his wrong. Legally speaking, he owed me and each of my brothers thousands of dollars in back child support. He wasn't helping me pay for college, but his finances were such that my younger brothers were not going to get the financial aid I was getting. After a few conferences with my mom, I approached my father with a deal: help my brothers go to college without complaint, give my mom the equity you own in our house, or I take you to court. And yes, I was willing to send him to jail. He agreed and kept his promises for the most part. He helped them with school. He complained and talked about how hard it was on him, but he helped.

The first semester of my sophomore year of college was over. As an R.A. (Resident Assistant), I was the last to leave the dorm for the semester. I was making a sweep of the dorm, checking the storage room, when I found myself getting teary. I sat on one of the dorm couches stored in the room and began to weep. Actually, I was crying like a little boy. I was grieving. My dad was gone. He still lived, the man who was once my dad. But he was gone. I was a man becoming, but had no one to follow. I was sure of my calling from God but had no one to mentor me. I was ashamed of myself for the relationship I had just gotten out of and had no dad to ask how to deal with it. No man to whom I could confess. No flesh and bone representative of God to whom I could confess. I was alone. At 19, I was a little boy, abandoned....still.

I cried out to God. Out loud, all alone. I pleaded for Him to take the pain, take the grief, take the hurt and make it right. I asked why? Why He had let me sin? Why He had left me alone? And why I had made such a mess of my life? I don't know how long I was there, but I do remember a call to break my vow. God wanted me to let it go, to forgive the one who had betrayed me, to humble myself and let my father off the hook. God called me to forgive the man I vowed I would never forgive.

So I tried. I told God I forgave my father. I told God I would not let my father control my actions, beliefs, hopes and self-image any longer. God knows I tried. And I meant it.

Very soon, however, I learned my first real lesson about forgiveness. Forgiving someone who has hurt you is not a single event or a one-time prayer. The job is not done just because you punch the clock. I thought I had it handled, had figured it out....I thought I was done and on my way to knowing God better, serving Him more faithfully and bearing fruit in ministry. I was right and I was wrong.

## *~ Junior (a man becoming) ~*

A few conversations with my father around Christmas, a phone call on my birthday and his, and regular attempts on my end to encourage him and help him feel good about the father he was being, convinced us both that all was well. This forgiveness thing wasn't so hard. We were good. I could live with this. Then the letter came.

Early in the first semester of my junior year of college, I received a letter from a Catholic Bishop postmarked in my home town. We weren't nor had we ever been Roman Catholic. When I was growing up, we hardly even went to church. As far as I knew, the only one in our family trying to follow Christ was me. I HAD been to a Catholic funeral once but I hadn't filled out a card. Getting a letter from a Roman Catholic Bishop made no sense to me. So I did what any self-respecting college student would do. I threw it on my dresser (several plastic milk crates piled on top of each other) and figured I would get to it later.

It was a Friday night. There was a big party in the off campus house in which I was living. It was a time in my life when I was not into partying, but I wasn't going to make a big deal out of the fact that my friends were very much into that sort of thing. MTV was on the television (volume turned down). A stereo was playing way too loudly. People were standing in line for the keg. Guys were trying to talk up girls....speaking loudly over the music. Cigarettes were being smoked, cards were being played and one young lady was crying in the corner because her boyfriend was flirting with another girl.

Maybe I was being self-righteous. Maybe I was just tired of the noise. I choose the latter. But I retired to my room. I slid the door closed, which muffled the sound, and flipped through a Sports Illustrated Magazine. When finished, I tossed the magazine onto my makeshift dresser. The letter fell to the floor. I picked it up and decided to open and read it. After all, it was a Friday night, I certainly wasn't going to study.

The letter informed me that my father was in the process of converting to Roman Catholicism. I harrumphed. It went on to say that upon his conversion, my father wished to have his new marriage sanctified (or some such word) by the church. In order for that to happen, because divorce is not accepted by the Roman Catholic Church, his marriage with my mother would have to be annulled. The Bishop was writing to all affected parties giving them a chance to speak into the process. Being one of the affected parties, I was asked to "speak into the process."

I lost it. I was enraged. How dare he! My father, not a religious man, was asking the Roman Catholic Church to declare his marriage with my mom null and void; thus making me, in the eyes of the Roman Catholic Church and the eyes of God as my father saw God, an illegitimate child.

These were indeed the first thoughts to run through my mind. Later I learned, through much study, that this is not the official view of the Roman Catholic Church with regards to children from an annulled marriage. However, it sure felt that way to me. While I was not upset with the Bishop, he asked me to respond, so I did.

I filled page after page with poison, venom, vitriol and hatred. I let that Bishop know who this soon-to-be-convert really was. I wrote, swore, cried and wrote some more. I shook my fist at God, took back the forgiveness I had given my father and let it fly.

I never sent the letter. But I decided that day I would never again nurture a relationship with my father. I decided to be distant, aloof and to use whatever he offered but never allow him to get close to me or any family I may have in the future. We would, from this day forward, be estranged...whether he knew it or not. He was living rent free in my head once again. He was hurting me all over again. He was betraying me. I was nurturing my anger and I didn't care. In fact, I liked it. It drove me. It formed me. It was an old familiar friend.

The following spring, I borrowed one of his cars for the weekend. It was the one my step-mother, Mindy, drove. I was going to visit a girl on her college campus a few hours south...it was the week before finals. I played nice, worked the system and got the car. When the weekend was over, I kept it. I didn't steal it; I just didn't take it back to my father.

A month later, after no attempts on my part to contact my father and no attempts on his to track me down to get the car, I stopped by his house to return the vehicle. God had been working in me. I had been working on myself. I realized how miserable I was becoming. I was an angry young man with a call on my life to serve the One who forgives all my sin. I had decided to have a man to man talk with my father; to get it all out on the table.

He was home and alone. He greeted me at the door. He said nothing about the car and asked if I wanted a "coke® or something." I declined and said I needed to talk. We sat down, each on a couch, a coffee table between us. I hemmed and hawed a bit and then just put it out there. I said, "We need to talk about our relationship. We need to just 'get it all out on the table.'" I expected a little resistance and I was prepared with a rebuttal. He said, "I think we should start over, forget the past, sweep it under the rug and start fresh."

My response? My rebuttal? "I can't do that. We need to talk about this." I don't know if there was more to the conversation or not. What I do know is this: once he realized our talk was going to be on my terms or not at all, he reached across the table, grabbed my shirt, dragged me toward the screened door at the front of his house, pushed me through it and said, "Then hit the f-ing gate."

I was incredulous, flabbergasted, appalled and disgusted all at the same time. This was not what I pictured. I pictured tears, some anger, more tears and reconciliation. I pictured a man becoming having a man to man with his father resulting in the renewal of a right relationship between son and father. I took the car.

I drove to my best friend's house. I knew his family well. My buddy wasn't home. His mother was. My fury was turning to tears as she came out the door. She asked what the matter was. I told her. Then she said the most insulting, horrible, difficult and wise thing anyone had said to me in my life. "Walker, you're gunna have to learn to love your dad for who he is, not for who you want him to be."

I played nice, acted appreciative and left. I drove away swearing, angry and humiliated. I felt betrayed not only by my father, but by my friend's mom. I felt betrayed by God. How could this happen? I was trying to do the right thing. Trying to be a 'stand up guy.' How could anyone not accept an honest attempt at reconciliation? All I wanted was for my pain to be acknowledged. Was I asking so much?

## *~ Lesson on becoming a man ~*

Terms are for surrender, not forgiveness. Preconditions for grace do not exist. In a treaty or cease fire…yes. In showing mercy and offering grace…no.

I wasn't done, though I thought I was. My 'stuff' with my father was not over. It took years before I actually "heard" what my buddy's mom and the "old guy" in Winter Haven had said. I was learning that forgiveness costs the injured party and cannot be given with terms. Freedom does not come from a truce, only from forgiveness.

## *Chapter 3*
# *"Prodigal Father"*

### *~ Steve, that hurt. Thanks. ~*

Having been thrown from my father's house and being informed I wasn't loving him in the right way, I took an opportunity to serve at a camp for a month between my Junior and Senior years in college. I needed to get away, refocus, pray and think. It was a volunteer position and while I needed the money that month of work would provide for college, I chose the volunteer position of "town runner" at the camp in northern Minnesota Oh, and by the way, the 'town runner' is a very nice term for camp errand boy. My job was to drive back and forth from camp to town to pick up supplies, keep the camp store in inventory, and shuttle people back and forth to the medical center when needed.

I knew I needed to get away. I desperately needed to spend some time with other believers, with God and with myself. It was a great month. In fact, it was one week in to that month when I learned a truth about myself that I have come back to time and time again. The summer staff was meeting on a deck overlooking the lake. Steve, the summer staff leader, was leading the devotions that evening. He read the following section of scripture and interrupted the reading here and there to explain, articulate and/or clarify the point. His interruptions (or my memory of them) are in italics below:

**John 5:1-14 (NIV)**

Some time later, Jesus went up to Jerusalem for a feast of the Jews. [2]Now there is in Jerusalem near the Sheep Gate a pool, which in Aramaic is called Bethesda and which is surrounded by five covered colonnades. [3]Here a great number of disabled people used to lie--the blind, the lame, the paralyzed. [4] [5]One who was there had been an invalid for thirty-eight years. [6]When Jesus saw him lying there and learned that he had been in this condition for a long time, he asked him, "Do you want to get well?"

*Steve: "In case you didn't know, there was a legend surrounding this pool. There is a reason the blind, the lame and the paralyzed used to gather here. The legend says that every now and then an angel would come and dip its wing into the pool, thus stirring up the waters. The first person into the pool after the waters were stirred would be healed."*

[7]"Sir," the invalid replied, "I have no one to help me into the pool when the water is stirred. While I am trying to get in, someone else goes down ahead of me."

*Steve: "This guy, this invalid had bought into a system that could not give him what he needed from it. The blind could hear the water stirred, get up and get in. The deaf could see the water stirred, get up and get in. This guy...this guy could see and hear the water when it was stirred but could not get up to get in."*

[8]Then Jesus said to him, "Get up! Pick up your mat and walk." [9]At once the man was cured; he picked up his mat and walked.

The day on which this took place was a Sabbath, [10]and so the Jews said to the man who had been healed, "It is the Sabbath; the law forbids you to carry your mat."

[11]But he replied, "The man who made me well said to me, 'Pick up your mat and walk.'"

[12]So they asked him, "Who is this fellow who told you to pick it up and walk?"

[13]The man who was healed had no idea who it was, for Jesus had slipped away into the crowd that was there.

[14]Later Jesus found him at the temple and said to him, "See, you are well again. Stop sinning or something worse may happen to you."

*Steve: "It seems funny to me that Jesus kind of yells at this guy. Notice he says, "Get up!" with an exclamation point. Maybe I'm wrong, but it seems like Jesus is a little frustrated with the guy." Of the group Steve asked: "Anyone have any idea why?"*

No one answered....we were college students but none of us wanted to be wrong. At least not in front of a bunch of other college students we barely knew.

*Steve: "Look back to the beginning of the story. What did Jesus ask this guy after he found out he had been in this condition for thirty eight years?" A student answered: "He asked him, "do you want to get well?"*

*Steve: "Exactly, and what was this guy's answer? Don't you think if Jesus asked you if you want to get well you should say, "YES"? But this guy doesn't; he gives all the reasons why he is NOT well. That wasn't Jesus' question."*

Steve then turned to me; he knew my name but didn't know my 'stuff.' He just knew I was a person who wasn't afraid to talk, an extravert. I have always been a group leader's best friend or worst enemy. When a question is asked, I usually have a ready answer--sometimes too willing to share and too long an answer. Steve turned to me and asked, "Walker, do you want to get well?"

Without hesitation and with anger dripping from my lips, I broke into a diatribe about how he doesn't know me, doesn't know where I come from or what I've experienced. I told him, overheard by the group, that I have tried to "get well," and there are some things that just can't be fixed. I've done what I needed to do and at this point it's in the other person's court.

When I paused and looked around, I saw nothing but blank stares, confused faces and regret on Steve's face. I realized I had ruined the time of devotions for the group and opened up a can of worms I did not want everyone…anyone, to see. I excused myself and walked to the beach. Steve finished up politely and came to apologize to me for putting me on the spot. We exchanged a few words and pleasantries and when he left, I knew I was the invalid. I, unable to walk on my own, had bought into a system that could not give me what I needed from it and when Jesus asked if I want to get well, all I could do was tell Him why I am not.

It was time; time to get up, pick up my mat and walk. It was time to stop sinning, before something worse happened to me. But how? How do you forgive a man who doesn't think he needs to be forgiven? How do I forgive my father when he won't even acknowledge my pain? If I forgive it without his acknowledgement, doesn't that just tell him what he has done and continues to do is OK? Even right?

It was decades before I could truthfully answer those questions. Stay with me, the first real epiphany is not far away.

## ~ *Father's Day* ~

Upon graduation from college, I took a position with Young Life Staff in the Chicago suburbs. Over the course of three years there, I became more and more fruitful in ministry, was certain of my calling, began dating and was engaged and then married to my lovely wife, Ellen.

As our time in suburban Chicago drew to a close, Ellen and I decided we wanted to consider starting a family. So from

Chicago, we began the process of looking for work around the town in which we attended college. Unable to find work immediately, we gave our notice to Young Life, said our goodbyes and moved back to Western Michigan. A few weeks later, I was in summer Greek class at a local seminary and had begun the interview process to be a youth pastor at a local church.

Summer Greek completed, a new calling secured, we settled in to our new life together. The weekend before we bought our first house, we found out we were pregnant with our first, Claire.

The next year had its ups and downs, but overall, things were good. Ministry was going well, our daughter was healthy, family visited, friendships were budding, we were blessed with a son, Scott and we were a family.

As youth pastor, I was often asked to give the children's message at one or both of our worship services. Our second year in the church I was asked to give a children's message on Father's Day. The topic: Ephesians 5:1 paraphrased says: "Imitate the Lord in all that you do, just as a much loved child imitates his father."

I knew for days what I needed to do. I'm one of those pastors who, as often as possible, especially when speaking with children, tries to use experiences from my own life to communicate the truth of the scriptures. I had one experience I could remember when I wanted to be like my father. One time I wanted to imitate him. I decided on Thursday what story I would tell.

The day before Father's Day my family and I went to see my father. Ellen had learned by now that I needed antacids before I visited my father. I was uptight and anxious, but it was what I had to do. I didn't want my new family to see the pain and betrayal in my life. I could suck it up, deal with it and soldier through the visit.

We were sitting in my father's condo with his wife and mother. As dinner was being prepared, my father was speaking to Ellen. I was in the other room, playing with the kids or changing a diaper. This was my strategy. When at my father's home, I would be attentive to my children and thereby be excused from having to participate in conversation any more than necessary. As they were talking, I overheard my father tell my wife that he had asked each of his boys to forgive him.

How the conversation lead to this 'revelation' I do not know. My wife has a way about her. People, even total strangers, are willing to share the most intimate details of their lives; both their fortunes and misdeeds. Her winsome spirit disarms. It is what drew me to her before we started dating. She just kind of sparkles; I have no other way to describe it. How the conversation worked its way to my father's confession, I do not know, but I do know he was trying to 'play' her. I had observed a pattern of behavior over the years; he desperately wanted people to see that he regrets his decisions and would often look for the chance to make himself look thoughtful and penitent. I don't know if he would have said the same thing if he knew I could hear. I don't know if he actually believed he had asked each of his boys for forgiveness.

Maybe he had asked my brothers and assumed he had asked me. But I KNOW he never asked me. I would have remembered it. It was what I had been craving, hoping and praying for the last 14 years.

I went to the car, grabbed a few more antacids and returned for dinner, playing nice, a little quiet and internally brooding. During the ride home, Ellen asked, "What's wrong? You seem quiet." I couldn't articulate it at that point. Everything, I mean everything was boiling to the surface. So I lied. I told her I was fine, just a little nervous about the services the next morning.

## *~ Underwear ~*

The children were gathered up front. With the microphone in hand I put on my best "talking to kids" voice and began with this story. "When I was a boy, my parents dropped my two brothers and me off at my grandma and grandpa's house. My little brother, Trip, was about to be born so my mom and dad had to go to the hospital for a few days. We stayed over-night and the next day, when it was time to get dressed, my grandma noticed my mom and dad hadn't packed any clean underwear for me." There were a few giggles and one child said to his brother, "he said underwear." More giggles.

The story continued: "My grandma said we had to go to the store to get more underwear. She said, 'we'll go to Kmart®.' But I didn't want to get underwear from Kmart®, I wanted JC Penny® underwear. When my grandma asked why I wanted JC Penny® underwear, I told her 'because that's the kind of underwear my daddy has.'

Still speaking to the children, I said, "See? I wanted to be just like my dad, even down to the underwear." I then made the connection between Ephesians 5:1 and God. Just as I wanted to be like my father, so we should want to be like God. Do any of the boys sitting here want to be like their daddies?" Nods. "Do any of the girls sitting here want to be like their mommies?' More nods and a few head shakes from the boys. "Just as we want to be like our parents because they love us, we should want to be like God, doing what He does....because He loves us."

Granted, this was not the most theologically or doctrinally complicated message I had ever given. Nor was it profound in insight and convicting of spirit, but it worked. The children were dismissed to their classes, I took my seat next to Ellen and I heard not one word of the sermon that followed.

When we got home, Ellen asked again if I was OK. I told her I wasn't. I said I felt dirty, like I had just prostituted myself by telling that story. I didn't like that everyone there assumed from the story that my father was someone I want to imitate. I didn't like that I had mislead people, especially in worship. While the story I told was technically accurate, I did want JC Penny® underwear when I was six because my father wore JC Penny® underwear, it just felt wrong.

Ellen tried to encourage me. She asked if there was more to it than the children's message. I confessed. I revisited the conversation she and my father had the day before. I acknowledged that he probably intended to ask for forgiveness but he had never asked me. Ellen suggested I call him and talk about it. I knew that wouldn't work. He would hem and haw and dodge the point. I had already been there with him and it ended in me being thrown out of his home.

So I sat, thought, prayed and stewed. Finally I told Ellen I was going to my father's house. We were going to play golf so I had him alone with no place to go. Ellen suggested I call him to make sure he was available. I told her if I called, he would have an excuse why it wouldn't work out today. I had to just show up. So I grabbed my clubs, called a friend to borrow his so my father could play and I headed to my father's house.

## *~ Get your smokes. You're going to need them. ~*

Unannounced, I arrived at my father's condo. Mindy answered the door. I told her I needed my father for a few hours, it was Father's Day after all. She acquiesced. I walked in and "surprised" my father. He greeted me with the standard greeting, "Hey bud."

"Hey" I said. With eyebrows up and a pleasant tone, I said, "We're going golfing, go change your clothes"

"But I don't have clubs, you know that."

"I've got clubs for you. I've covered all the bases. My treat. Go change. What else are you going to do, sit and watch the Tigers get beat again?"

He said, "But..."

Interrupting him, I said that which you never say to your southern raised father, "Just shut up and go change. We're going golfing."

He changed, kissed his wife and followed me to my truck.

When he got in my truck, I said, "Go grab your smokes, you're going to need them." I was playing with him a little bit. He claimed to have stopped smoking but we (his sons) all knew that he kept a pack in the car so he could smoke when driving and running errands.

He said, "You know I quit those things a year ago."

Again, I said something I had never said to him before that day. "Just shut up and go get your smokes, you are going to need them. Otherwise, we'll stop on the way and buy some more."

He got out of my truck, went to the garage and came out with a pack of smokes. By this time, he was getting wise to the fact that this wasn't about golf, though he had no idea what was coming.

When he closed the passenger door of the truck, he asked, "What's this all about?"

I did not know this is what I was going to do, though it is something I should have done years before. I said,

"Yesterday, you told my wife you had asked each of your boys to forgive you."

He interrupted, with a little panic in his voice. "That doesn't mean you have to."

"Shut up and let me finish." His eyebrows raised in disbelief. I was pushing the "shut up" thing pretty far.

I continued. "You never asked me."

He looked down, hung his head low.

"Today is Father's Day and I don't have a present for you, but I do have a gift. I give you my forgiveness. From this day forward, I will no longer hold against you the things you have done or have not done to and for the family. I forgive you for leaving me, divorcing me, abandoning me, for not paying child support, for putting me between you and my mom. I forgive you for all of it. It's a clean slate. I will do whatever I can to treat each thing that might come up in the future as if it is a *new* thing. The old is gone the new has come. I give up the right to hold the past against you, to pull out my baggage and to remember whatever has happened in the past whenever something new takes place."

He wept.

I drove.

We played golf.

On the seventh or eighth hole, we actually started joking and talking. He asked if there was anything I wanted. I told him I just wanted him to arrange a time, a weekend, where the two of us could get away and just be father and son. A fishing trip, a ballgame, it didn't matter what we did. I just wanted my dad and wanted to be his son. He promised. I made it clear there was no time limit. It didn't have to be now. I just wanted him to know I wanted that experience....with him.

We completed our round of golf, I took him home. His smokes *were* gone. We were both spent. I drove home.

## ~ *Faith Lesson: Forgiveness is a gift.* ~

You may have noticed up to this point in the story, my father had yet to acknowledge to me that he needed my forgiveness. He had yet to acknowledge he had done wrong or caused me any pain. It was this very fact that finally motivated me to give him a gift...to forgive him. Forgiveness is for giving, not for receiving, not for seeking acknowledgement of my pain and certainly not for getting something in return.

I am not the sharpest knife in the drawer but I am no dull blade either. It took my adolescence and into my early adulthood to realize this simple truth. Forgiveness is not just for the benefit of the perpetrator of wrong; it is (maybe more so) for the benefit of the person wronged.

## *Chapter 4*

# *"Some time later, God tested..."*

Recently, while listening to sermons of pastors we were considering for call to our church, I heard a pastor say, "God does not test us." I could not disagree more. I knew I had been tested….had been tested by God. In fact, this pastor was dead wrong according to the witness of scripture. The first line of the familiar story of Abraham sacrificing Isaac starts like this: "Some time later, God tested Abraham."

If you are unfamiliar with the story, you can read it below with my commentary (in italics). If you would like to read it in its entirety without my commentary, you can find it at the beginning of the Bible in the book of Genesis, chapter 22.

**Genesis 22:1-18 (NIV)**

[1]Some time later God tested Abraham. He said to him, "Abraham!"

"Here I am," he replied.

[2]Then God said, "Take your son, your only son, Isaac, whom you love, and go to the region of Moriah. Sacrifice him there as a burnt offering on one of the mountains I will tell you about."

*In other words, "Take your son, the one that you waited a lifetime for, the one who is the guarantee of the promises I have made to you, the son that you would die for, the one who makes your heart swell with joy and pride, take him to Moriah and slaughter him there, for Me."*

*God spoke audibly to Abraham and told him to do something wicked. "This is not the God I know. Only the pagan gods require human sacrifice. How can this be God's voice?" Place yourself in his shoes. What would you think? Who would you tell? How would you sleep?*

*Everything God had promised, everything that God is had just been contradicted. God said, 'murder your son…for Me'?*

[3]Early the next morning Abraham got up and saddled his donkey. He took with him two of his servants and his son Isaac. When he had cut enough wood for the burnt offering, he set out for the place God had told him about. [4]On the third day Abraham looked up and saw the place in the distance…

*Three days had gone by. What would he talk about? What was his attitude? Was he praying that God would change His mind? Was he doubting his sanity, " Why is this happening? Why me? Why this? What am I doing?"*

...[5]He said to his servants, "Stay here with the donkey while I and the boy go over there. We will worship and then we will come back to you."

*Did Abraham believe this? Did he really think that they would come back together? Did he still have hope? Was he still doubting himself and what he heard? God had promised him this child, and that this child would be the beginning of blessing for all creation, could God take back a promise?*

[6]Abraham took the wood for the burnt offering and placed it on his son Isaac, and he himself carried the fire and the knife.

*The silence must have been deafening.*

As the two of them went on together, [7]Isaac spoke up and said to his father Abraham, "Father?"
"Yes, my son?" Abraham replied.
"The fire and wood are here," Isaac said, "but where is the lamb for the burnt offering?"

*Ouch! How could he respond to this? His heart was breaking, and his child, whom he was going to kill was asking him, "what is going on?" Was Isaac getting the picture now?*

[8]Abraham answered, "God himself will provide the lamb for the burnt offering, my son." And the two of them went on together.

*More silence!*

[9]When they reached the place God had told him about, Abraham built an altar there and arranged the wood on it. He bound his son Isaac and laid him on the altar, on top of the wood. [10]Then he reached out his hand and took the knife to slay his son.

*How far would you go? ...Really. Think of Hebrews 11 and its account of Abraham being a hero of the faith. If the story had stopped there, Abraham would have been remembered as a psycho, not a hero.*

> [11]But the angel of the LORD called out to him from heaven, "Abraham! Abraham!"
> "Here I am," he replied.
> [12]"Do not lay a hand on the boy," he said. "Do not do anything to him. Now I know that you fear God, because you have not withheld from me your son, your only son."

*The connotation for "fear" here is not so much "frightened of" or awe, but willingness to be obedient even to the point of killing your son. In essence God said, "You were willing to give up all that I have promised you, all that you live for, all that is dear to you, for me. Because you were willing, keep it, hang on to it, live in it and rejoice."*

> [13]Abraham looked up and there in a thicket he saw a ram caught by its horns. He went over and took the ram and sacrificed it as a burnt offering instead of his son. …

*God sent a scapegoat: a creature that takes the place of the people of God in a sacrifice. The offering demanded blood, and God provided it. Sound familiar?*

> … [14]So Abraham called that place The LORD Will Provide. And to this day it is said, "On the mountain of the LORD it will be provided."
> [15]The angel of the LORD called to Abraham from heaven a second time [16]and said, "I swear by myself, declares the LORD, that because you have done this and have not withheld your son, your only son, [17]I will surely bless you and make your descendants as numerous as the stars in the sky and as the sand on the seashore. Your descendants will take possession of the cities of their

> enemies, [18]and through your offspring all nations on earth will be blessed, because you have obeyed me."

Would God ask you or me to do anything like this now? I don't think so. But neither did Abraham. It is absurd and makes absolutely no sense at all. But just how far would you go?

There was a student who came to Socrates as the philosopher knelt by a stream. The student posed the question: "What is truth?" Socrates immediately grabbed the boy and held his head under the water until he began to struggle furiously. Then Socrates pulled him up and said, "When you want knowledge the way you just wanted air...then you shall have it."

Is faith like air to you? Is it something that you crave like a baby craves mother's milk? When people lose everything, they learn what is important. Mother Teresa once said "You'll never know that Jesus is all you need until Jesus is all you have." This, Abraham was willing to discover, but I'm not sure that I am. When tested, I fall short every time. I am not worthy of the love of God because I am not willing to give everything to Him.

If you are like me then remember one thing. The next time God doesn't make sense, the next time life hurts, the next time it looks as though in order to follow God you must give up all that you are, remember Abraham. He was obedient and God gave him back everything that he was going to give up and more. God is a jealous God. He wants our lives. He wants to be our Lord. He wants us to serve Him. To do this is to be obedient even when it doesn't seem to make sense.

# *~ God Tested Me ~*

I tell you this story because it was something I had been learning, a chapter I had been translating, a sermon I had been preparing just before I went to my father's condo to 'play golf.' I forgave him that day, but I had no idea how difficult it would be to live that forgiveness. There was no context in which to place the next few years. In my mind, forgiveness was given. I had made promises to my father and I would keep them. Done. End of story.

That summer, just a month or two after Father's Day, I lived out my forgiveness. And I was tested in it.

Since before my daughter was born, I had privately vowed that my father would never have any real influence over my children nor would I ever truly trust him with them. I know. This sounds awful and non-Christian but it is the truth.

Ellen and I were taking a group of high school students from our church out to Colorado for a week of adventure: white water rafting, rappelling, rock climbing, etc. Because it was a trip for high school students and we were traveling via church bus, there was no way for us to travel with our daughter, Claire. So, after much discussion…OK, to be fair, it was mostly me arguing with myself out loud to Ellen…we decided to ask my father and his wife, Mindy, to take watch of our daughter while we were gone.

This would be the longest we had ever been away from Claire…nine days total. To be honest, I'm not even sure she had been away from us overnight before. And it would be a test. While it may not seem like a big deal to others (leaving a daughter in the care of her grandfather and his wife who were perfectly capable of caring for a fifteen month old for a week) it was to me. It meant living what I had promised. It meant feeling as if I were betraying my mother who had expected to be asked to take care of her granddaughter and who had never played second fiddle to my father when it came to Claire. It also meant I had to sacrifice something I loved. No, not my daughter; my bitterness, my anger, even my hatred.

You see? For years I had nurtured my wounds, treated them with the finest ointments, but kept them just short of healing. My injured, abandoned-little-boy identity. My angry-young-father mentality. My need for justice and the retribution owed me had become old, dear friends. I knew them well and they knew me. I could always count on them and they always knew how to make me feel 'better.' It sounds sick, but ask anyone addicted to cigarettes why it is so hard to quit. They will tell you the nicotine addiction is one thing, the habits are another. The cigarettes are always there for you. They calm you down when you are stressed. They keep you company when you are alone. They share meals with you. They join you on road trips, at meals. They have been at every party, every funeral, every joyous and every painful occasion. In a way, smokers don't know how to be themselves without cigarettes. In the same way, I didn't really know how to be me without anger and resentment. I didn't know how to be well. I had finally arrived at the pool of Bethesda. Jesus had asked, "Do you want to get well?" And I had answered, "Yes." But, just as the invalid in John 5 must have had trouble adjusting to a life of productivity instead of a life of begging, I needed to learn to be well. I needed to live forgiveness. I was being tested.

Did I really forgive my father if I didn't live as if he were my dad? Could I say he was forgiven and not entrust to him the child I loved dearly, my daughter Claire? Was I willing to sacrifice my identity, my need for justice, on the mountain?

My mother understood and supported the decision. We dropped Claire at my father's home and left for Colorado. We didn't have cell phones at the time, so communicating with Claire was sporadic. We managed, then we returned.

My father, his wife and Claire met us at our little house. Claire was reluctant to come to us. We had been warned this might happen, since she was only fifteen months old and her attachments for the last two weeks had been with my father and Mindy. As she came closer, we saw a black and swollen eye. My little girl, whom I love, had been injured while in the care of my father and his wife. Don't read this wrong, there was no abuse; no harm done to Claire intentionally…that never even crossed my mind.

My father was timid and apologetic. Mindy was given the task of explaining what had happened. Claire had fallen while playing and hit her head, her eye on a coffee table. Ellen looked at me, my father looked at me, Mindy looked at me….what would be my response?

My heart hurt. My little girl was hurt. She hardly recognized me, and all this while in the care of my father. I was tempted. I was tested. I could go back to being the person I was or I could crave faith like it was air and trust God like Abraham. I could "get up, pick up my mat and walk" or I could continue to explain why I wasn't well.

Did I pass the test? I don't know. I said what needed to be said…. "Things happen, it could have happened when she was home just as easily as it happened at your house, etc." But it didn't go away. I chewed on it, thought about it and wrestled with God regarding it for weeks. I don't remember all the prayers but I do remember one. "Lord, why can't this be easier?"

Remember Abraham? Do you think it was easy for him? Remember the invalid at the well? After thirty eight years as an invalid, was it easy for him to step back into his family, find a job, renew his identity as a productive member of society? If I romanticize these people and assume all went well for them and everything worked itself out like the application of a sermon or the last three minutes of a sitcom, then yes. But if the scriptures are real, if they depict real people in real life, then I have to believe there is more to the 'stories' than are recorded in the text for us. Abraham was human and he loved his son. Isaac was human and he loved AND TRUSTED his father. The nameless man, only known for his infirmity, was human. Life was difficult and his healing, his new self, who he was in Christ, must have been tested.

## ~ *Passed the Test?* ~

I would love to tell you this was the only test of my forgiveness. It was not. I learned some things over the next two years I hope I never forget. The tests were frequent because my father was still my father. The tests were continual because I was not yet the man God wanted me to be. Yes, I had picked up my mat and was walking, but my legs grew tired. I was learning to live with a new identity, a man who forgives, but my skills needed honing and practice. I needed discipline and the Lord gave me ample opportunity to practice. I had been trying to live forgiveness like a person who tries to run a marathon. Trying is very different than training.

## *~ Lessons learned in the fire ~*

1) *Forgiveness is giving up my right to hold "it" against the perpetrator anymore. It means each time something comes up, it comes up for the first time…and the last. Forgiveness says, "You hurt me. What you did hurt ME. However, from this point forward, I give up my right to hold it against you."*

The statement above does not mean you forget "it" happened. It does not mean what was done to you did not hurt you. It does not mean what was done to you was OK or right. It means you have decided not to withhold this from God. It means even *this* can be redeemed. It means Christ died for the sins committed against you, just as He died for the sins you have committed.

I have heard the Lord's Prayer (or the "Our Father" for my Roman Catholic friends…including my father) recited three different ways. There is little difference in the recitation from one denomination/tradition to the next, but where they differ, a new connotation is noted.

> "Forgive us our sins as we have also forgiven those who have sinned against us"
>
> "Forgive us our debts as we have also forgiven our debtors"
>
> "Forgive us our trespasses as we forgive those who trespass against us."

They are all faithful to the Greek (the original language of the New Testament). In fact, all three words/ideas (sins, debts and trespasses) are needed to get an accurate sense of the intended meaning. When someone sins against us this is what is taking place: the one sinning has decided to consider his/her desires or needs above yours. Therefore he takes something from you....he lessens your worth, leaving him in your debt. He walks property upon which he has no permission to tread, thereby trespassing.

2) *Until I am willing to give up that which I desire, I may never receive it. And giving up that which I desire is no guarantee I will ever receive it. If it were, I have not really given it up.*

Abraham was willing to go farther than I would ever consider. He did not KNOW the Lord would not require him to actually murder his son. He may have hoped, but he did not know. Only after he 'passed the test' did the Lord give him what he desired, a scapegoat, one to die in the stead of his son. I wanted acknowledgement of my pain. I desired confession from my father. Since the day he told me he was leaving until the day I returned from Colorado, I wanted him to admit he had sinned against me, was in my debt, had trespassed on my identity and person. This chapter ends two years...two years after the day I forgave my father...and I had yet to hear one word of acknowledgement. Gratitude for my forgiveness? Yes. Appreciation for our developing relationship? Yes. Acknowledgement of my pain? No. And I was OK with it. Truly.

I was, and still am, becoming a man who forgives simply because I am forgiven by God.

## *Chapter 5*

# *"Full Circle.....Almost"*

In a previous chapter, I mentioned God's work in me as it pertained to needing to forgive my father whether or not he ever acknowledged his need for forgiveness. In addition, my forgiveness, in order to be legitimate, had to be tested...could I live as if I had forgiven my father?

Before I tell you the story about events that took place two full years after that Father's Day when I forgave my father, I want to share one of Jesus' parables with you. While I would love to tell you I read this parable, pondered it, prayed over it and then decided what I must do--offer forgiveness--that simply wouldn't be true. The truth is this parable began working on me as I began working to become a man who lives forgiveness. The subtleties of the meaning became more and more obvious to me as I began helping others learn to forgive their fathers, girlfriends, spouses and friends.

Again, my commentary is in italics below. Please pick up a bible and read the passage uninterrupted by my commentary before proceeding.

**Matthew 18:21-35 (NIV)**

Then Peter came to Jesus and asked, "Lord, how many times shall I forgive my brother when he sins against me? Up to seven times?"

*Peter's question comes just after Jesus informs Peter that whatever he forgives (looses) on earth will be forgiven (loosed) in heaven and whatever is not forgiven (bound) on earth will not be forgiven.*

22Jesus answered, "I tell you, not seven times, but seventy-seven times.

*There was a Rabbinic (Jewish pastors) tradition of forgiving someone who sins against you seven times. Seven is a number of completeness and this tradition was considered exceedingly gracious. However, Jesus tells us grace is much more gracious than we expect.*

*If you are counting in your head (seventy one, seventy two, etc), you can stop. The number seventy seven implies infinite completeness, not just a large score card.*

23"Therefore, the kingdom of heaven is like a king who wanted to settle accounts with his servants. 24As he began the settlement, a man who owed him ten thousand talents was brought to him. 25Since he was not able to pay, the master ordered that he and his wife and his children and all that he had be sold to repay the debt.

*Let's take a second to consider the numbers in this passage. First of all, 10,000 was the largest number in the first century. There were no millions, billions or trillions. Ten thousand was the MOST. Therefore, in this parable, when Jesus uses the number 10,000 talents, it would be similar to you or I speaking in billions or trillions.*

*A talent consisted of between six and ten thousand denarii. A denari was an average daily wage for a laborer or employee. So, today, if the minimum wage were $7.00 per hour and a person worked eight hours per day the worker would earn approximately $56.00 per day. Being conservative and using the low end of the value of a talent (6000 denarii) in today's dollars, Jesus was saying the servant owed the master $3,360,000,000. This is obviously no personal loan. In fact, it is not even back taxes. This would represent approximately nine lifetimes of wages for a typical worker. In other words, in this parable, Jesus is using unfathomable numbers to make his point.*

[26]"The servant fell on his knees before him. 'Be patient with me,' he begged, 'and I will pay back everything.' …

*An impossible task. It's unthinkable to even ask for patience and claim to be able to pay it all back.*

… [27]The servant's master took pity on him, canceled the debt and let him go.

*I'm sure you see this without me telling you, but just in case....If the kingdom of heaven looks like this: the master represents God and the servant represents me and you, the fact that God would be willing to cancel a debt that CANNOT, under any circumstances, be repaid is a picture of both grace (getting what I don't deserve) and mercy (not getting what I do deserve).*

[28]"But when that servant went out, he found one of his fellow servants who owed him a hundred denarii. He grabbed him and began to choke him. 'Pay back what you owe me!' he demanded.

*The contrast here is astounding. The very servant who was forgiven nine lifetimes worth of wages demands repayment from a guy who owes him just over three months pay. Was it owed him? Of course. Should it matter? Not after the master forgave his debt.*

*Granted, we are dealing with money in this parable, but before you read on, take a look at the sins committed against you. What is it you are angry about? Who is it you can't (can't is just Latin for won't) forgive? Does he owe you an apology? Does she owe you an acknowledgement of your pain? Of course. So what is Jesus getting at here? Doesn't it seem that Jesus is saying, "You have been forgiven a debt that could not, under any circumstances, be repaid, why won't you forgive the one who hurt you?"*

[29]"His fellow servant fell to his knees and begged him, 'Be patient with me, and I will pay you back.'

*This 'fellow servant' did exactly what the first servant did with the master in the parable. He begged, completely at the mercy of the one holding the debt.*

[30]"But he refused. Instead, he went off and had the man thrown into prison until he could pay the debt. [31]When the other servants saw what had happened, they were greatly distressed and went and told their master everything that had happened.

*Whether he was owed payment or not, if you were the master in this story, how would you respond when you learned the one you had forgiven much had not forgiven little? Would you not be irate?*

[32]"Then the master called the servant in. 'You wicked servant,' he said, 'I canceled all that debt of yours because you begged me to. [33]Shouldn't you have had mercy on your fellow servant just as I had on you?'...

*Remember, this IS a parable about forgiveness. This IS what Christ expects from us. In Jesus' words, this IS what the kingdom of heaven is like.*

... [34]In anger his master turned him over to the jailers to be tortured, until he should pay back all he owed.

*The easy point first: how was this servant going to pay back all he owed if he was in prison? It couldn't be done. Now the hard one: the master handed him over to the jailers to be tortured. Would God do this? I thought God was love. Patient. Kind. See Jesus' next line for the answer.*

[35]"This is how my heavenly Father will treat each of you unless you forgive your brother from your heart."

*Where is the jail or prison where the servant will be tortured? Remember, this is a parable. It is a story used to illustrate a point. My experience is this: the jail and prison are my own mind. All that time I spent not forgiving my father, all the years of anger, all the 'head' time given to contemplation and accusation was for naught. The only person suffering from my unwillingness to forgive was me.*

*If you have been hurt, no matter what the source of the pain: betrayal, theft, abuse, violence, humiliation or being treated like a thing instead of a person, the only person hurting as a result of your holding on to and nursing that grudge is you. While the one who hurt you may not care IF he knew how bad it hurt, fact is, he probably doesn't even know.*

It was my mom who learned this lesson and passed it on to me. It just took longer to take root in me than it did for her. She met a man who had been betrayed by his best friend. They were partners in a business and his friend embezzled hundreds of thousands of dollars from the company and then left him to pay the debts and work to re-claim his good name.

In a lodge in northern Minnesota, this man was telling his story. When finished my mom asked him how he could be so calm about it. The man responded with something like this: "What good will it do me to be angry? My ex-partner doesn't care…he doesn't even know, the only person who cares or knows is me."

## ~ *Issumagijoujungnainermik* ~

No, the heading above is not a meaningless jumble of letters accidently appearing on the page because the author fell asleep on his keyboard. Try to sound it out: I-sue-maaji-jouw-jung-naner-mik….at least that's how the author pronounces it.

When the Moravian monks took the Gospel to the indigenous people of Alaska, they found the native people did not have a word for forgiveness in their language. The monks, after learning the indigenous language, constructed a word using known vocabulary. The attempt, though lengthy, was noble. The word Issumagijoujungnainermik transliterated means: not-being-able-to-think-about-it-any-more.

When you consider the scriptures that speak of God's forgiveness of our sins, be thankful that God decides to "remember your sins no more." He decides to not be able to think about them anymore. I'm not saying God forgets, I am saying he chooses to remember them no more. Here is the challenge: God wants us to do the same. Can you forget the event(s) that caused you pain? No. Can you forget the suffering, humiliation, victimization? No. However, you can choose to dwell on these things no more. There is an old proverb, the origins of which I do not know, that says: "You cannot stop a bird from flying over your head, but you can keep it from making a nest in your hair."

I can't forget the betrayal and abandonment of my father. I can choose to live in such a way that I do not obsess over it. I can choose to work at becoming the man God wants me to be, instead of dwelling on the man I might have been if my father hadn't left me. Pain can be either a healer or a crippler, depending on how it is treated. Ignored, it will paralyze and fester. Faced and forgiven, it can break chains, free slaves and lead to a better understanding of and relationship with God.

It wasn't until I began to understand, live and teach this truth, willing to live with never receiving from my father what I wanted most from him, that I received it. While there may not be a clear Biblical truth in this statement, nor a parable or Bible story (Abraham and Isaac maybe), I have found this to be a way God works in my life and others. Until I am willing to live without something, I do not receive it. I cannot manipulate God by feigning willingness to do without. Until I am willing to offer my desire as a living sacrifice, I am left in want. God calls us to do some very difficult things, the hardest of which is this: dying to self. I have to be willing to give up my rights before God gives to me the very thing I have been holding out for. I had to give up my right to be angry and bitter toward my father before I began to experience freedom from self torture. In addition, I had to be willing to live without my father's acknowledgement of the pain he caused before I received the acknowledgement I needed. I gave up the right to have my need fulfilled.

## *~ Promise Keepers ~*

As promised at the beginning of the chapter, there is a 'conclusion' to the story of reconciliation with my father. You will notice after this story that I no longer refer to him as my father, but as my dad.

In the early 1990's there was a movement in the US, a revival of sorts. The movement was known as Promise Keepers. Certain groups and media outlets called it 'controversial,' but most of those people had decided they knew what it was about without actually *knowing* what it was about. Boiled down, Promise Keepers was a movement calling men to be men of God, to keep the promises they had made to their wives, children, church and God. For the most part, the movement consisted of rallies or stadium events. There was follow-up material and men's groups which started up in many churches, including ours, but for the sake of this chapter, the stadium events were the big draw.

After hearing of these Promise Keepers events, a buddy of mine, Steve, and I went to Indianapolis for one of the Promise Keepers rallies. We stayed with another friend who lived outside of Indy in Zionsville, IN. We attended and had a great experience. The worship was amazing, the speakers great and the experience of 60,000 men together praising God was astounding. The following year I decided to take my brother-in-law, Mitch, my brother Randy and my father. While I was surprised my father was willing to come, I tried to keep a low profile about it. He had recently begun to speak of his faith pretty openly. Through his conversion to Roman Catholicism he had come to a saving knowledge of Christ.

Randy, Mitch, my father and I headed to Indianapolis. We stayed with John in Zionsville. The first night was good. The music was amazing, the teaching good but I got worried near the end of the evening. The preacher, a famous evangelist's son, did what I thought was a less than spectacular job with his call to Christ. When he began to ask men to come forward and give their lives to Christ, I expected to see no one go forward. I certainly don't want to come off critical here, but I must say I had heard hundreds or thousands of Gospel presentations. I had seen dozens or hundreds of calls to the altar. Never had I been so amazed at the response to the Holy Spirit in spite of the presenter. When the hundreds or thousands of men began to move forward, my father leaned to me and said, "I didn't expect anyone to respond to THAT." I laughed out loud.

The next day's topic concentrated on passing the blessing from one generation to the next. The single men were asked to join the other single men in a different area. Randy joined them. In our section of the RCA® Dome, were my father, John, Mitch, me and about four hundred other men. As the speaker began to talk about blessing your sons and grandsons, I began to get a little antsy. I was with my father and two other men whose stories were similar to mine but worse. Mitch, who was in his mid-twenties, had only recently met his biological father for the first time. John's father had been inept and absent. Three men in one row who had never experienced the blessing of a father....one of them sitting with his.

John Trent, the speaker, after several minutes opining on generational blessing, instructed anyone there with their sons or grandsons to rise, to stand with their sons and grandsons. So everyone who represented generations together in Christ was to stand. The implication was, "See how these men are blessing their offspring...one generation to the next? What a glorious thing God has done through all of you." In our section, my father and I were the only ones representing generations of men. At the instruction to stand, we stood. Then the explanation of what this meant was given. There was no way I was going to sit back down. It was a time to really live the forgiveness I had given. As the other men in our section gathered around us to pray over us, lay hands on us and thank God for the great works He had done, I felt peace. My father, in front of all these men, got to be proud of the blessing he had been to me. I hoped he knew what I was doing for him, by remaining on my feet but even if he didn't, it was OK.

After the prayer time, after the other men from our section of the stadium returned to their seats, John Trent shifted gears. He began to speak of surrogates, of men taking the torch dropped by others, of the need for other men to bless the sons of others who were abandoned, left behind or abused. I could see what was coming next. Anticipating the awkward moment's arrival, I began to sweat in my seat. My father was sitting immediately behind me. We were in the upper level, so his seat was slightly raised above mine, I was leaned over as if in prayer. But I was not praying, I was fighting with myself.

John Trent continued, with something like this: 'Stand up....If you grew up without a father. If you never knew him.' Mitch stood up. 'If he was abusive or inept, or spiritually vacant and unavailable.' John stood up. 'Even if he was around but not really there, if you knew him but weren't known by him, if he divorced your mother.....' I didn't know what to do. I looked over and both Mitch and John, who knew my story...all of it, were looking at me. The question in all of our minds was, "what is Walker going to do?"

My father and I had just been prayed over by hundreds of men. Everyone in our section assumed my father had worked hard to leave a Godly legacy to me, had passed on a blessing. They thought I knew the Lord because my father had been a man of God. That's what the prayers said. Many of them assumed my father brought me to Promise Keepers, not the other way around. *How can I stand? He will be humiliated. How can I stay seated, I'll be lying? What's the right thing to do?* I just didn't know. My decision? Protect my father's reputation with these other men. Give him what he may not have deserved but live like he did...all these thoughts ran through my head in seconds. I turned my head and made eye contact with Mitch and John one more time. I 'half-grinned' at them, knowing they knew what I had decided. A little proud of myself and a little 'spent' by the emotional turmoil of the last several seconds, I bowed my head again, this time to pray.

I felt a touch on my shoulder. It was my father, thanking me for not embarrassing him. *I can live with this. He knows what I just did for him and is saying thanks.* This is good and right. Then there were hands under my armpits, lifting. I resisted. Turning around, I saw my dad leaning over, hands under my arms LIFTING me up. Surprised, without a word, I inquired...what are you doing? He just smiled and placed his hand on my shoulder.

He had finally acknowledged my experience...my pain....my suffering...my story...my life as I had lived it. That which I wanted most my dad gave to me that day. Later, we talked. He knew. He had. He did.

## *~ Faith Lesson from The Keeper of Promises ~*

God said to me through this experience, "Now that I know you honor me because you did not withhold your need from me, your major need, to be acknowledged by your father and blessed by him, you were willing to forgive as I forgave you, you were willing to die to self to save your father's reputation, your father is now your dad. While others thanked God for the blessing your dad had been to you, you remained quiet. Then, when you were afraid you would embarrass him in front of those men, I prompted him to bless you. He lifted you up. He acknowledged your pain. He died to self for you."

We had come full circle....almost. Sixteen years had passed since that day my father told me he was leaving. This day, my dad blessed me. Act 1 was complete. The antagonist in Act 1, the first sixteen years? Him. The antagonist in the next Act? Me. Read on, please.

## *Chapter 6*

# *"An Old Friend Pays a Visit"*

### *~ Progress ~*

The next several years went well. My dad got to know my wife and kids. We talked, visited and shared experiences. It wasn't perfect and I came to realize it would never really be the way I hoped it would be, but I came to grips with it and was resolved to let it be what it was.

A few years after the Promise Keepers experience in Indianapolis, IN, my dad, his wife and my half-sister moved to Valdosta, GA. My dad had been offered a new job down there and since his bankruptcy several years prior, the salary would help regain some of the losses experienced and begin the process of building toward retirement. He built a wing on his new house that would allow for visits from his sons and their families. We visited them a time or two and had a pleasant time.

In the late 1990's Mindy was diagnosed with cervical cancer. She was desperately ill and I was able to work out a time to visit them before she died. Mindy was a good person…and 'no' I'm not just saying that because she has passed away. It took a long time for Mindy and me to get past the harm done to our family, but over time I came to see what my dad saw in her. She was good for him and was very helpful to me in my coming to understand the Roman Catholicism my dad had accepted as his faith. Mindy and I often talked, in depth, about things spiritual, her family and mine, about her pain and mine. She had become a good and dear friend.

When she died in January 1999, I went south for the funeral. My dad asked me to deliver the eulogy – a summary of Mindy's life and the legacy she was leaving. There was some irony in this but I agreed. I worked hard to learn of Mindy's life with her family of origin, was honest about my relationship with her and with the blessing she ended up being for me, my wife and kids. After the funeral, people gathered at my dad's home. Sitting outside with my dad, next to his pool, each with beer in hand he said something I will never forget. In his southern gentleman drawl he looked across the patio table and said, "The Good Lord put two wonderful women in my life. One I treated like sh**, the other…..I did OK."

Wow! I had never heard him say this or anything like it. I was amazed and once again blessed by my dad. I hoped he would one day tell my mom the same thing he had just told me, but what I just heard was enough.

## *~ Satisfaction ~*

On Easter Sunday that year my dad called my mom. He called for one purpose, to apologize for what he had done to my mom and to ask forgiveness. Ellen, Claire, Scott and I, were in Boston at the time, visiting Ellen's family. My mom called me to share the content of my dad's call. She and I were both a bit flabbergasted and befuddled. My role in the family had not changed. I was still the confidant to my mom and dad, the go-between, even the arbiter of motives and 'keeper of family lore.' I know that sounds a bit arrogant and I write it tongue in cheek. Our family system had found a balance. If there was a story, experience or decision that affected my whole family of origin, chances were I was in the loop. If questions arose concerning facts or truth, of motive or intent, I seemed to be asked my opinion. When my mom informed me of the call she had just received from my dad she was wondering if she was being 'played.' She wanted to believe it was genuine but was looking for some sort of confirmation. I shared with her what my dad had said by the pool after Mindy's funeral. Satisfaction.

The first thing that went through my mind after I hung up the phone? Maybe my mom and dad will get back together. I was thirty three years old, my parents had been divorced for more than twenty years, and the first thought that went through my mind was of reconciliation? No wonder God says He hates divorce in Malachi 2:16. He knows the yearnings of the soul and the long lasting wounds not only for the husband and wife but for the larger family. I knew this was childish and next to impossible, but I still thought it and still hoped....maybe....maybe it could happen. My hope did not last long. Nothing difficult or wrong happened, I simply allowed myself to be thirty three again instead of twelve.

## *~ Orlando Part 1 ~*

In November 2001, we took the kids to Disney World® in Orlando, FL. This was our second trip to this Mecca of consumerism and pleasure, but we liked it. The kids were getting a little older, so the "It's a Small World" ride could be bypassed and replaced with "Pirates of the Caribbean" and "Space Mountain." Ellen's mom and dad had a time-share and had invited us to join them at a condo development instead of adding the expense of staying in the Park. We accepted their offer. My mom was invited and Ellen's brother, whom we call Curley, joined us as well.

As I remember it, I started the vacation frustrated. I had planned a vacation with just my wife and kids. Somehow there had been a 'pile on'. Who's to blame? I don't know. But here we were; our nice, quiet, immediate-family-only vacation in Orlando with my mom, Ellen's parents and her brother squeezed into a time-share condo meant for four. My desire was to create family memories with the Dee family...just us. But while frustrated, I could deal with it. Until.....

Ellen's parents are very, very generous people. They had, on more than one occasion, offered their home, time-shares, etc. to members of my extended family. This experience was no different. They knew my mom and treated her very well. They also knew my dad and treated him with the generosity that oozed from them all the time. Being retired and equipped with a motor home, they had occasionally stopped by to visit my dad and Mindy before she died. Somehow (and it might have been from me) my dad had learned we were going to be at Disney®, only four hours from Valdosta, GA. He decided to join us one day with my half-sister, who was three years older than Claire. Everyone seemed to think this was a great idea. Everyone except me.

Please keep in mind that while much reconciliation had taken place in my family of origin, and forgiveness had been asked for and given between my parents, there had never been a time since the separation that my parents were in the same place at the same time which was not torturously awkward and uncomfortable for me. Barring my wedding and the weddings of my brothers, I could not remember one time we were all together that ended well.

Much of my life as a son had been devoted to duty to my mom: making sure she was never left alone on a holiday for more than a few hours as we headed off to see my dad; ensuring she always knew the appreciation I had for her unwavering commitment to me and my brothers. Every opportunity as it was presented, I chose to honor her over my dad, not out of spite toward my dad, but out of reverence for my mom.

She had forgiven him, but he was the last person she would ever have chosen to spend her vacation with. And here we were, in Orlando answering a call from my dad that he planned to meet us in the park and spend the day with us. Ellen's parents were thrilled. Everyone spoke of how nice it would be to have him join us. I looked to my mom. She chose to be classy about it and just stay quiet. I was livid. My mom had been invited to join us and now she was going to have to deal with my dad in order to spend time with her grandchildren. I could take it no more.

I sat the adults down in the living room of the condo and told them this was unacceptable. Ellen's parents were taken aback because they had known nothing of the story between me and my dad and my mom, only that everyone seemed to get along just fine at the weddings. Bless their hearts, they thought much more highly of the Dee's than we deserved. My mom offered to stay at the condo the next day so that I wouldn't feel awkward. It was just like her….sacrificing her own desires for the sake of one of her sons. Unacceptable! She had spent a lifetime making sure we could know our dad. She had spent hours alone on holidays and birthdays to make sure he was honored. I could not allow her to sacrifice here so my father could play grandpa. Yup. You read it right, I called him my "father." My old, dear, horrible friend had returned. His name? Anger Bitterness Painful Wounded, II.

I'll leave it at that. My kids didn't know how we dealt with the stress. They had a great day in the park as did my mom, dad, Ellen's parents and brother. I 'cowboyed' up and dealt with it. But I didn't do surgery. I didn't have the energy. This injury would pass.

## ~ *Orlando Part 2* ~

Things progressed as you might imagine. Within eighteen months of Mindy's death my dad was remarried. A year later he and his new family moved to a suburb of Tampa, FL. We had some contact, but not much. We were not estranged again, just busy with life. My kids had soccer, volleyball, baseball, etc. and I was pastoring a young church plant. My dad had three teenagers in the house, a new wife and was beginning a real estate career. He called on birthdays, holidays and whenever he needed me to fix one of his computers remotely. Overall it was a pretty normal adult-child and parent relationship. I didn't hate him. I liked his new wife. We had settled into a relationship that was both tolerable and mutually beneficial.

You may remember, in one of the previous chapters, the day I forgave my father and he became my dad I told him I wanted him to set up a time where the two of us (just the two of us) could go fishing, golfing, to a ball game....something like that. That day was more than a decade behind me. I had not forgotten the request but I had resigned myself to the likelihood it would never take place. My assumption was that he had forgotten all about it. It was likely a much more meaningful request to me than to him. In his defense, I had downplayed it and put no strings on it. It was just a request, and of all the things that happened on the golf course that day, this request was the least important.

Ellen's parents wanted to take us to Orlando again, a different time-share resort with lots of activities. They wanted us to do what we wanted when we wanted to do it; Disney®, swim, visit friends, fish, etc. They paid for us to fly down. Our kids (one teenager and the other getting close) had some friends who had moved to the area and they wanted to visit. This vacation sounded great. As it turned out, two of my brothers, Randy and Trip, were going to be in the area as well. For a long time, Trip had been my fishing partner. We talked and decided it would be a great chance to go fishing on Tampa Bay for saltwater gamefish. I spoke with my father-in-law and asked if he was interested. He was. I called my dad and told him my father-in-law, Trip and I would like to take him fishing. He sounded excited. I asked if he would be willing, because he was local, to research the best fishing guides and reserve the day. He agreed and found the guide.

We arrived in Orlando, solidified the fishing plans and packed our gear the night prior to the day my dad, father-in-law, brother and I would all go fishing together. Sitting out on the deck of the condo, sipping on a beer and talking with my son, I felt my cell phone buzz in my pocket. I checked to make sure it wasn't someone from church interrupting my vacation. It was my dad. I answered the phone and got quiet for the next five minutes. The guide was set, the fishing looked like it would be good the next day, he gave directions to the marina and told me he wasn't going. There was an important phone call he needed to be able to take if it came.

I asked, "Do you have call forwarding on your business telephone?"

"Yes" he answered.

Having fixed his computers many, many times I asked, "Do you know how to use it?"

"Yes."

"Just set up the call to come to your cell. If you get the call, we'll stop whatever we're doing until you are finished. We can even head back in early, if you need to deal with something."

He said what I knew he would say, "I'll feel more comfortable being at home if the call comes. Ya'll have a great time. Stop by the house when you're done and tell me all about it, we'll order pizza."

We ended the call. There was a tsunami of questions, feelings, hurts and betrayals. The next five seconds lasted ten minutes in my mind. *I come eighteen hundred miles and you do not come visit me and your grandkids. How cheap can you get? I'll pay for you to go fishing with two of your sons. Please come fishing. Call back. Say you're sorry. You SOB. I should have seen this coming. What the hell is wrong with you? What did I do?*

I stayed stoic on the surface but Ellen had overheard. She came to the deck and asked what the matter was. I told her he was not going fishing us. She asked why, and I told her it was because he was expecting (or hoping) for an important phone call. She hugged me. My son, Scott, who was still sitting on the deck with me asked. "Dad, why doesn't your dad want to spend time with you?" I looked him in the eye tenderly and said, "Scotty, I don't know."

Wounded anew.

*********

I realize how pathetic this might read. However, as a pastor I can tell you my experience is not an isolated one. The wounds inflicted, intentionally or otherwise, by a parent to a child are as chronic as HIV/AIDS. The illness looks differently on/in each person, but there is nothing that can be done, barring supernatural intervention to rid your body (in the case of HIV/AIDS) or soul (in cases of parent/child) of the virus. The innate desire of a son or daughter to be approved by his or her parents is God given. This is one of the reasons God reveals Himself to us as Father, Abba, Daddy, Papa.

*********

When this new wound was inflicted, it didn't hit me like a twelve year old boy. It landed on a thirty eight year old soul. It bounced on the psyche of a man, not a child. I knew who I was and knew I had no 'claim' on my dad. I was happy with who I was becoming and saw this as an opportunity, though a painful one, to continue to live the forgiveness I had given.

My father-in-law, Trip and I went fishing. And other than the unbelievably foul mouth of the guide, we had a great time and have since often spoken of the great memories of that day. After a long hot day of fishing on Tampa Bay, we went to my dad's home for pizza and told him of the day we had.

He never received the call for which he had been waiting.

# *Chapter 7*
# *"Harbinger"*

## *~ Another Father's Day ~*

Sunday, June 17 was Father's Day in 2007. Personally, I struggle with "Hallmark®" holidays. I like to think it is because of principle, but more likely than not, it is due to my thoughtlessness and unwillingness to look ahead on the calendar. Nevertheless, Father's Day was the third Sunday in June, just like it always is. I got up early, went to my office to put the final touches on my sermon, worshipped with the congregation, preached at both services, and later in the afternoon, headed to Trip's house to spend some time fishing on the river.

Trip and I didn't talk much. It's not that we didn't like each other, it's just that brothers (or maybe men) fishing together don't usually look at the time in the boat as an opportunity to share intimate details of our lives, but to *not* share intimate details of our lives. Hanging out fishing is the point, not talking. OK, back to the point. After fishing an hour or two, Trip turned his head toward me and asked, "Did you call Dad today?" I paused and then answered honestly, "Nope."

I knew it was Father's Day. My kids and wife had given me a card and a gift. People at church had wished me a happy Father's Day and I them. While I hadn't preached about fathers, it was obvious it was Father's Day. I found it interesting, as I stood in the boat, it had never even occurred to me to call my dad….never even crossed my mind. *What kind of a person am I? Who doesn't think to call their dad on Father's Day? I don't want to call him. I should call. I'll call him on my way home...maybe. Why don't I want to call?*

We finished fishing. I packed up and started home. Honestly, it never crossed my mind again. I didn't call.

The next day, while emailing a member of our church whose kids had done something very nice for him on Father's Day, it occurred to me again that I had forgotten to call my dad. I sent him an email. After two days, no response. I left a voicemail….no return call. Throughout the summer, I tried a few other times to get in touch with him, but to no avail. This was, as it turned out, to be the longest time he and I had had no contact since the summer he told me to "hit the gate."

# *~ In Me ~*

It didn't bother me much…that we didn't talk. As I look back, I can give him credit I was unwilling to give him then. I'm sure he didn't take my missing Father's Day too hard. After my attempts to contact him, I'm sure he thought to himself "I'll get back to him in a little while…when I get home….when it's not so late…I know he's busy." It had been the height of the Real Estate boom in Florida and he had been busy.

As I said, it didn't bother me much. Our relationship was more a surface friendship than it was a dad and son relationship anyway. However, when I did think of it, I thought of it in a rather negative way. I assumed he was making me pay for forgetting to call. Now and then I would talk to Ellen about it. I told her this was a trick I had never seen before. In the past, I controlled how often we talked or visited. My dad made few, if any, demands on my time. In truth, I didn't know what was going on. I was confused. I wanted him to know I meant no disrespect toward him when I didn't call, but was kind of amazed at the fact that I had simply forgotten. There was no play book for that summer. I didn't know if he was angry or distracted, nor did I know if I was being passive aggressive or just forgetful.

Looking back, I should have seen this as a harbinger of things to come. Something was changing in the relationship between my dad and me. There was something both new and difficult just around the corner.

## *~ Counsel of a Friend ~*

I have a friend who lives in California who is one of the few people with whom I am completely honest. Glenn is a friend in the truest sense of the word. He is honest with himself, willing to accept correction, likes to argue for the sake of arguing, and is a rock. I trust him. I share my sin, faults, neuroses, joys and disappointments with him.

That summer I made a mistake. I told him about forgetting to call my dad on Father's Day and my dad's lack of response to my efforts at contact. Glenn asked a follow-up question that escapes my memory at the moment, and I took the bait. As the conversation continued, I shared with Glenn that I wondered if my dad was having marital problems. I told him I had heard from Randy that my dad often complained about how his wife treated him. Glenn asked if I was going to talk to my dad about it, if I was going to try to help my dad. My response was, "Nope."

Glenn set out to correct my attitude and wrong behavior. While there was a dose of arguing for the point of arguing, there was honest concern for me as well. He spoke to me of doing what was difficult instead of what was easy. He talked to me about how I valued the marriage relationship, instituted by God. He was smart; every argument he made was an argument he had heard me use. He even reminded me that "foolish is the man who will not take his own advise."

I argued, at first in fun, then in earnest. I joked about being foolish and just played the game for a while. Then he pulled out what we lovingly refer to as "Number 5," the fifth commandment: ***Deut.***

***5:16 (NIV)*** *"Honor your father and your mother, as the LORD your God has commanded you, so that you may live long and that it may go well with you in the land the LORD your God is giving you."* In the moments that followed I became a person I did not want to be, I began to be a person who argued technicalities in scripture. I knew Glenn was right, but didn't want him to be. I argued that my father was not really my father if he had not lived up to his responsibilities as such. Yes, I was supposed to honor my dad but he was supposed to be honorable. Yes, I was commanded to respect my dad but I had been more a dad to him than he had been to me. I went on and on.

Glenn apologized for touching a nerve and confessed he was just in an argumentative mood. However, when we were finished with the conversation, I sat down on the couch in my office and grieved. At first, I grieved the loss of not having the dad I had always wanted, then for how quickly I was willing to disobey a command from scripture, and later for how short of the mark I had been as a father to my own children.

## *~ Background Music ~*

As I write this, I desperately want to 'save face' with you (the reader). I want to remind you that I am choosing to "tell on myself," showing you the rooms in my head that aren't on the normal tour. The contents of this book and these stories I tell are not the sum total of my life, nor are they consciously driving forces day to day. They are more like background music in a movie. The music sets the mood, tries to convey emotion and gives you subconscious clues that something is coming, that all is well or be afraid…be very afraid. When watching a movie, I have no control over what music is playing, but I can decide to pay attention to it and see how I am being influenced. In my life, sometimes the music is loud, other times it is soft and sometimes I am better at paying attention to it, realizing how it is influencing me, than others.

*********

Please know two things: 1) I am telling on myself because it is the truth and 2) I am ashamed these things have taken so much time and joy from my life.

## ~ *Already/Not Yet* ~

As the summer continued I spent time praying through my stinkin' thinkin'. I confessed, grieved, sought forgiveness and moved on. I was beginning to come to grips with the likelihood that I would never truly recover from this loss in my life. I knew I had made progress but understood clearly that I had a long way to go. This journey was not over and God was beginning a new work in me. The scripture passage that kept coming to mind was Philippians 3:16 (NIV), "Only let us live up to what we have already attained."

In Christ I was forgiven. My heavenly Father was the only dad I really needed. These things were *already* true but in me they were *not yet* a reality.

## *Chapter 8*

# *"This One's On Me"*

### *~ Coming to town ~*

Trip and I were in his dining room getting ready to go fishing for what would probably be one of the last times of the season. It was the first week of October 2007. While I was trying to clean up his wife's laptop computer, my dad called. I overheard the conversation…one side of it. Turned out my dad was coming to Michigan for a visit the last week of October.

Trip said, "hang on, I'll ask," turning to me and asked, "Are you preaching October 28?"

"Nope," I responded.

Back to the phone he said to my dad, "Nope."

The conversation continued and Trip gave me a look, rolled his eyes a bit and put one finger in the air as if to say, "I'll tell you in a minute." The conversation ended and I asked Trip why he wanted to know if I was preaching on the twenty eighth. He knew, though likely didn't remember, that I had taken that Sunday off because we were planning to move my mom out of the house we had grown up in. We had been working on her for years, trying to convince her she needed to sell the house and move into a condo, or at least a smaller home. It was just too much for her to keep up because the house was almost 140 years old. We had finally convinced her and the house had been sold. This was going to be difficult for her, and us, as there was a lot of history for our family in that house.

We had moved there from Southern Georgia in the early 1970's. After my father left the family, that house was where my mom made a life for herself and her boys. Everyone in the community knew it was our home. My mom had lived there for almost thirty five years. All of her sons were going to be there to pack, move and remember.

Trip told me my dad had asked about that weekend because he was coming north for a visit.

"Doesn't he know we are moving mom out of the house that weekend?" I asked.

"He knows," was Trip's response.

"What is he thinking?" I asked.

"I don't know." Trip said.

Internally to my dad...*Don't you realize how difficult this is going to be for her? This is the house you two bought together and planned to raise your family in. Not to mention the fact that you are going to be in town to "visit" and none of us are going to be available. This is the last weekend you should be coming.*

"Why did he want to know if I was preaching on the 28th?"

"He said he was going to come hear you preach." He paused and rolled his eyes.

"What?" I said with a sarcastic tone.

"When I told him you weren't preaching he said, 'I work it out to come all the way up there to hear him preach and he's not preaching!?'"

With a knowing grin to Trip and a facetious tone I said, "Yea, I've been preaching weekly for over nine years, he's never come to my church much less heard me preach, and he thinks I scheduled a Sunday off because he planned to come."

"He also wants me to buy a lotto ticket for him." Trip said this because he knew it would make me laugh. It had been a running joke between the two of us. My dad would ask Trip to buy a multi-state lottery ticket for him whenever the jackpot rose above 100 million. He would ask Trip to keep it a secret saying, "If we win, we'll sort it out later."

I laughed as I was expected to. Trip had always been the one in the family who hates conflict and is gifted in relieving tension.

As I mentioned earlier, while fishing, Trip and I seldom talked about anything that mattered. There was a little friendly competition and he usually won. We would ask about each others' kids and such but for the most part, it's just two brothers fishing and not talking about anything that mattered...just the way we liked it. I had some time to think. I was wondering which of my brothers told my dad that I was a little hurt he had never come to my church. We had planted this congregation nine years prior and had started it with nineteen people between the ages of nineteen and twenty five, and it had grown to average weekly worship of around six hundred people. I should have known better than to share things like this with my family members because they usually took it upon themselves to pass on the frustration or disappointment. I don't know, maybe I wanted them to. I wanted my dad to come hear me preach but I also reveled a bit in the fact that he never had. While I wanted him to see me…see what the Lord had been doing through me, I also liked the fact that he had never been there, because it confirmed in me my view of him.

Don't get me wrong here…I have always loved my dad. I have always desperately wanted him to be proud of me, not just say he was proud of me. I wanted him to approve of my life's work. I wanted his love. However, if I am honest with myself, I don't know if I would have really received it if he had given it. In a way, I was twelve years old again. In a way, I was an adult child of an imperfect man who was resigned to the fact that this was just how it was going to be.

The thing that bugged me was that my dad had picked THAT particular weekend to 'come hear me preach.' I assumed he knew I would be helping my mom move. I assumed he chose to say that was the weekend he wanted to come to my church because it was an easy out for him. He could look like he wanted to come but not actually have to show up. All this was going through my head as I was fishing with Trip. He kicked my tail in our friendly competition….as he usually did.

I went home that evening and told Ellen what was going on. She said, "T" (that's what she calls me) "I'm so sorry. Are you OK?"

"I'm fine." I lied. It bugged me and I was disappointed in myself that it bugged me. I thought I was beyond this. I had forgiven him. I had been wounded anew but each instance, each event, each wound was to be treated like an isolated incident. *Why did I give him so much power in my life? Why was I so concerned about this? Who cares? Why am I hurt that he is coming when I am not preaching? Why does it bother me that he is coming on a weekend when we (my brothers and I) won't be able to spend much time with him? Why am I giving him so much prime real estate space in my head? He's living rent free again.*

## ~ A Weekend in October ~

As it turned out, my mom had not yet closed on her house and therefore we were not moving her into her condo that last weekend in October. The preaching schedule was set, however, so I still had that Sunday off. On Saturday Randy, Trip, their families and my dad came to our home for pizza and a visit. We, as usual when my dad was around, didn't do anything accept turn on the TV to watch whatever game happened to be on.

As a side note, I don't watch sports. I have nothing against them, I simply find watching sports on TV kind of boring. So these family gatherings are both awkward for me, due to the family dynamics at play, and boring.

Everyone was pleasant if not predictable. My dad asked about the kids, commented on how fast they were growing up, asked about my church and expressed how disappointed he was that he was not going to get to hear me preach.

I played the good soldier. I answered his questions about the kids, said I was sorry about the preaching schedule but explained it was put in place long before I knew he was coming to town, and ate more than my share of pizza. However (and this was new in me), I was tempted, while he was asking about my kids, to ask him if he even knew their middle names. I don't know why. Part of me just wanted to create in him some of the feeling that was beginning to well up in me again. I wanted him to know how disconnected he was from his family, just as I felt and knew how disconnected I was (and my kids were) from him. But I soldiered up and played nice.

Nearing the end of the visit, Randy asked Trip and me if we were still planning to come to his house on Monday. It was mom's birthday and he was hosting the party in his new home. We all confirmed we would be there and secretly handed Randy the money we owed him for the gift we were pitching in on.

Overhearing the conversation, my dad began to speak. Unbeknownst to me, part of his reason for visiting that weekend was that he had some business to do in northern Indiana. It was part of the project he had been working on for years and was indeed related to that important phone call he never received a few years back when we were supposed to go fishing. While in the area, he was staying with Randy and his family. He said, "On Monday, ya'll don't worry about me." It had never occurred to me. "Ya'll go ahead with the party. I'll probably be in Elkhart, but if that falls through, I'll just find something else to do. I'll go get a bite to eat or just drive around for a few hours. Your momma deserves to have her party. I don't want to get in the way." We all nodded and said that was very gracious. To be honest, I don't think it had ever occurred to any of us that he would be anywhere near Randy's house during my mom's party. But I was relieved after the fact that he had seen the potential difficulty and had a plan.

I was pleasantly surprised. He was being considerate of my mom and willing to catch a movie or something so she could be with her boys and their families. Wow, maybe all the real estate he had been given in my head was for naught. Maybe he was more altruistic than I thought. This was pretty big of him. I realize now that I was putting a lot of weight on this very small gesture, and I know putting this weight on this small gesture was doing the very thing I thought it wasn't. I was once again paying his rent for him while he lived in my head. The difference this time was that I was willing and ready to make said payment….to pay his rent, because this was the second time in my experience that I had seen my dad consider the larger picture and decide to paint himself out of it.

## ~ *The Call* ~

Sitting in my office on Monday morning having just finished with two hour-long staff meetings, my phone rang. It was Randy. He was calling about my mom's birthday party. I asked if my dad was in Indiana. He told me the meeting had been cancelled, and after a pause, that my dad was going to be at his (Randy's) house during the party. Out of my mouth, without any forethought, having not engaged any kind of filter, I blurted out "No he's not!"

The conversation continued. Randy was in a tough spot. Since my dad had said he was going to stay in the house, Randy was left with two options: 1) Call everyone, including my mom, to inform us so we could prepare ourselves for an awkward night and play nice, or 2) Ask my dad to leave. Randy could not bring himself to "kick my dad out of my house." I understood. I had been trying to do that in one way or another for almost thirty years. I didn't say that to Randy but I certainly understood the predicament in which he found himself. He was going to have to ask my mom to bend, share and compromise once again so my dad wouldn't feel unwanted or uncomfortable. This was Disney World® all over again, except it was happening to all of us, not just me.

As the conversation was coming to an end, I told Randy I would have to call him back in an hour or so because I was not sure I would be able to attend the party any longer. He didn't know all the baggage I was carrying but he knew I carried it in a very different way than he did. He was gracious and said he understood. My parting comment was simply this: "The last place on the planet dad should be tonight is at the birthday party of the women he left. Doesn't he GET THAT?" Randy's response? "Apparently not."

I sat for a while and stewed. I walked down the hall to talk to my friend, the church's youth pastor. He listened and commiserated. I called Ellen and told her I couldn't go to the party and why. She understood.

I needed to take a stand. To say, "not this time, you're not ruining this for my mom…for me." I wanted my brothers to tell him why I wasn't coming. I wanted him to know. I wanted him to feel bad. I wanted real estate in HIS head. (Wow, I'm a jerk.) This would only draw attention to me. This would do exactly what my dad was doing…take the attention off my mom's birthday and put it on me. Crap. I had to go. I called Randy. I called Ellen. They understood.

## *~ The Party ~*

On the way to Randy's house…about a forty minute drive…I continued to stew a bit. I couldn't get past how inappropriate it was for my dad to be at my mom's birthday party. *Doesn't he see what he's doing? Doesn't he remember what he did to her? What? He can't go catch a movie? Visit old stomping grounds? Call a friend he used to hang out with? Go for a walk? For God's sake, be anywhere but Randy's house tonight.*

I hoped he would 'get it' and I took another antacid. Over a decade prior, I had forgiven my father. He had become my dad. My best friend's mom had been right. I had needed to learn to love my dad for who he was, not for who I wanted him to be. Our relationship had grown. It would never be what I wanted it to be and if it could become something more, I'm not sure I wanted that either. Things were tolerable, livable….they were OK.

*******

I don't want to give the impression that I thought about my relationship with my father/dad all the time. I didn't. However, I know my experiences in that relationship drove me, molded me, changed me and (in many ways) made me who I was. I didn't obsess over it, but when it reared its head I changed.

A friend and colleague of mine brought this to my attention previously. After a prayer session he asked if I had a few minutes. This colleague was a new pastor at our church and was quickly becoming not only a dear friend, but a pastor to me. During the prayer time, I had talked about the conversation I'd had with Trip after my dad called and found out I wasn't going to be preaching on the Sunday in

October. Sitting in his office, my colleague, my friend, my pastor said to me, "I don't want to over step my bounds but I want to tell you something."

"Shoot"

"I hope you can find resolution and healing with your dad."

"I think I already have."

"I know you say that and I believe you. However, as we have gotten to know each other I've seen your heart. You are compassionate and passionate. You care deeply for others…you are grace-ful. But when you talk about your dad….you're a different animal."

"Really? How so?" I asked with all sincerity. I thought I been covering it pretty well. This took some guts on his part, because I was his boss, but I deeply respected his willingness to push me.

He went on to tell me how I was different, that I was angry whenever I spoke of him, that there was little grace and much judgment. He was very pastoral in his approach and I was ready to hear it. And he was right.

*********

As we pulled in to Randy's driveway I was disappointed to see my dad's rental in the driveway. I resolved to do what I usually did when I felt awkward at family gatherings…I would just be the fun uncle and play with the kids. My nephews and nieces called me Uncle Tickle. If I were going to be a "different animal," I would be a cuddly one.

The evening progressed much as I expected. Greetings all around. Pop and appetizers abounded. My dad stayed on one side of the room, my mom on the other….for a while. I played with the kids, asked about school, tickled, teased, asked them to give me "five" and acted like they hurt my hand. I listened to bad knock-knock jokes, saw several Lego® creations and 'artwork' done in school. And I listened to the conversations going on among the adults.

I hate to write this because there is a chance my dad will one day read what I am writing, but what I heard made me feel sick to my stomach. They were talking about my mom's house which turned the conversation toward the Real Estate market in West Michigan, which was rapidly going the wrong direction. My dad, who was in Real Estate in Florida, began to share his expertise. For half an hour the conversation became about him. I tried not to be angry…a different animal…but I lost the battle. I continued to play with the kids.

At dinner, it happened again. I don't remember how, but we were talking to my mom and somehow the conversation came around again to my dad and his expertise in another area. I quietly excused myself and went out on the deck. My mom came out a few minutes later and I apologized to her for leaving dinner and for my dad being there. She assured me it was OK. She was fine and said how sorry she was that I felt awkward.

*What is wrong with me? I'm not really angry anymore, but I feel sick. Something has changed between the ride here and now.* I felt sad; hurt a little, but mostly sad. It may have had something to do with the fact that we all knew my dad was ill. He didn't know it yet, but we could all tell. He was thin…too thin, and he had a lump on the side of his neck. He had assured us it was just a gland that swelled up now and then. And he believed this to be true. But we knew it was more than that. Everyone had encouraged him to get it checked out. He had promised he would. Subconsciously, my melancholy disposition may have had something to do with this but not consciously. For the first time in my adult life, at least for the first time I could remember, I felt something and didn't know why.

I went back inside, played nice, and endured the evening. On the way home I told Ellen I was in a bit of a funk and I didn't know why. She asked about it, but we got nowhere. I informed her I needed to spend some time thinking and praying and I would let her know whenever I discovered what was going on inside of me. Graciously, she didn't ask me about it again for several days.

As the next few days progressed, I went from sadness to pity. Not self-pity, but pity for my dad. I did not believe this was a healthy place to stay, but it was a new place to visit for a while. *Why do I pity my dad? Why aren't I angry? Why aren't I reacting like I always have? Why can't I predict where this is going?*

Sitting in my office with a man about my dad's age, hearing his story of divorce, leaving his kids, feeling estranged from them and desiring to re-establish a relationship with them, I heard myself giving the following advice. "I encourage you to try. Take it slow. But keep in mind your kids are adults now. They don't need the daddy who left, they have other needs now. They have kids, jobs, spouses. And they may not feel the need to re-establish the relationship the same way you do. Make yourself available to them and respond with grace if they are not initially receptive. They will learn your motives over time. They just might not trust them yet." There was more to the conversation and more to my pastoral advice, but that summary should help you see what happened in me next.

As the parishioner left my office, I sat down and prayed. It didn't take long for me to realize….I assumed righteous motives in my parishioner but wrong motives in my dad. This man wanted to re-establish relationships with his grown kids. He missed them. Felt bad for leaving them. Wanted them to know. Needed them to know. In fact, he needed *them*.

He made mistakes. Did wrong. And needed grace. I encouraged him to seek it. Would I have given the same advise to my dad? Did I assume righteous motives in him? Could I see my dad as a man with regrets? Could I allow him to be repentant? Awkward? Needy? Or would I always assume he was selfish and hurtful? Was he a child of God or just my failed father?

I went home to talk to Ellen. I explained what happened in my time of prayer and contemplation. I confessed I had never seen my dad from my dad's point of view. The relationship with my dad had always been defined by my need for him to see my point of view, but I had never treated him the way I wanted him to treat me. Until these newer wounds and my mom's birthday party, I had been satisfied with the relationship, status quo, but had never considered.....he might not be. We (Ellen and I) talked and I began to look at things from my dad's perspective. He lived six states away from each of his four boys. His daughter had just left for college. He was in a marriage that he complained about all the time. His business venture didn't seem to be developing the way he would want. He was his wife's assistant in their Real Estate business. He was lonely, regretful, a little depressed, and was likely afraid he had cancer, but didn't want to go to the doctor for fear he might be right.

To Ellen I said, "If you were regretful, depressed, lonely, sick, had nothing going your way in your career, were in your mid-sixties and realized three of your four sons, three of your four daughters-in-law and six of your eight grandkids were going to be in one place, where would you want to be? Wherever *they were*, right?" She nodded.

I had no idea if these were the ideas my dad had going through his head, but it changed me. I was becoming a different animal. He was no longer living rent free in my head, demanding I pay his rent. He was "convalescing in my home" at my invitation. I began to care for him, instead of caring about him. I began to become an adult child to a dad with needs. I moved from pity to compassion and I am ashamed to admit, it had never occurred to me before.

The first fourteen years after he left were on him. He wronged me, left me, and abandoned me. It cost me and it cost me dearly. Forgiving him for his wrongs was a price I had to pay because it was a debt he could not cover. The first fourteen years....that's on him. The next fourteen years? That's on me. I forgave him but never saw him. I let him off the hook for what he 'owed me' but assumed he still wanted me to keep on paying rent for him. He went from father to dad but I never let him be daddy. He, like me, was a needy man with regrets. While I pray my kids will be compassionate toward me for whatever wounds I inflict upon them, I never allowed myself compassion for my dad. I had never seen his need, only mine...I had become just like him.

## *~ Darkness ~*

Two weeks later, he called. The diagnosis for the lump in his neck was stage-four squamous cell cancer on the base of his tongue. Surgery, chemotherapy and radiation were needed immediately. And it was dark.

# *Chapter 9*
# *"Four Days"*

## *~Cancer ~*

I've been a pastor long enough to know the evil that is cancer. You can judge a tree by its fruit. When the diagnosis is received there is disbelief and fear. While there are many cancers that respond well to treatment, the treatment, in and of itself, is painful, long and difficult. I have yet to meet a person diagnosed with cancer who doesn't both resolve himself to "beat this thing" and simultaneously "get his house in order." Fear, sickness, strife, pain, nausea, uncertainty, hopelessness, weariness and despair - all fruits of evil. All spiritual symptoms of cancer.

## *~ Now What? ~*

When my dad was diagnosed with cancer, I was forty one years old. I was finally figuring out I needed to not only behave differently toward my dad but think differently about him. I realized, in one way, I had become the very man I vowed never to be. I had become like my father; considering my needs, not the needs of others. With new found resolve, I was going to be a son to my dad instead of waiting for him to be a dad to his son. But how? My old friends - bitterness, unforgiveness and the keeper of grudges - had been sent packing. I had no frame of reference, no experience with my dad to help me be his son, his friend, even his pastor.

After his diagnosis, we talked a lot.....A LOT. I finally understood what other people in my small-group were talking about when they spoke of having the same conversations over and over with their parents. I heard about the upcoming surgeries, doctors' appointments, treatments, symptoms, and my dad's commitment to 'beating this thing' a dozen times in two weeks. I was asked to keep my brothers informed. I even began to develop a relationship with my half-sister. She was scared. She didn't get along very well with her step-mother, and after losing her mother to cancer when she was nine, the idea of losing her dad at eighteen was just short of paralyzing.

My dad, a southern man through and through, decided he needed to 'be strong' for his daughter. Translation: don't keep her informed about what is actually going on because it might scare her. Along with fear as her constant companion, she was angry with our dad. After a surgery to remove several tumors in his throat, he looked awful. She thought it was going to be a minor procedure and when she went to visit him, he looked like he was on his death bed. She was hurt and very, very afraid. At my dad's prompting, I called her. She trusted me with her feelings. I told her why he was being that way and we shared some newly discovered inside jokes about my dad. This was the first time I saw her as a sibling rather than a niece.

Three days later, after my dad was home and recovering, I made a call. Here I was; calling my dad to help him be a better dad to my sister, whom I hardly knew. With her permission, I shared with him what she was going through. I spoke to him about my daughter (3 years younger than his) and what she needed from me and would need if I were ever in his situation. I was parenting my parent. He actually listened. He needed to know…she needed him to know. He sat her down. They spoke. He apologized. Things got better. I had suddenly become what so many of my friends had become….a tweener. I was parent to my kids and 'parent' to my parent. I wondered, "When did I become normal?"

All these years I had hoped my father would know how much I needed him. I missed that. I grieved that. I was angry about that. I am done with that. Now I realize something I should have seen years ago. He needs me. I don't mean this in a sick or pathetic sense. My dad needs me just as I need my kids. My life would be significantly lessened if I were ever estranged from either of them. God forbid I ever have to bury one of them. I know my kids need me, but I need them. While I wish my dad had been the man who stepped up in my life when I needed him, it never occurred to me that he needs me. He needs my understanding, my wisdom, my acceptance, my forgiveness, my compassion and yes, on occasion, my instruction and guidance. I don't think I am better than him, I just know he counts on me for certain things. There are some things I see differently than he does, and some areas in his life for which he will seek (and accept) my advice. As I look back over the years at some of the phone calls I have received from him, I remember him seeking wisdom. Yes, it's clear that he needs me when his computers are broken, but he needs my help with parenting, too. He has called to ask how to keep his kids from feeling entitled, spoiled, etc. He doesn't usually listen to my advice, but he has always asked for it.

In this instance, with my sister, he listened. He listened because he knew (to some extent) the estrangement from him I had felt and because he knew I dealt with people in familial estrangement often. He could be a better dad to his daughter because I was his son. Redemption?

## ~ Florida ~

*I didn't realize it until I typed the name of the state above, but I find it interesting that so many of the watershed events in my life, as they pertain to my dad, have something to do with a state I have almost no connection to. This has nothing to do with the story at hand, but it will let you see a little bit of the random way my brain works.*

*********

After the surgeries, radiation and chemo-therapy began simultaneously. The first round of chemo, he said, was a piece of cake. By the third round, he said, "First I thought I was gunna die, then I was afraid I wouldn't." In my life, I had often heard him complain, but I had never heard him sound either weak or afraid. I knew most of the time, it was just bravado, but to hear him speak of the desire to die shook me. I called Ellen and the chair person of our church council and told them I needed to go south to see him. Randy and Trip would be down there for vacation in a few weeks, but he was afraid and lonely. His wife was around, but eight weeks caring for my temporarily invalid dad would be enough to drive anyone crazy. Plus, she had to get back to work. They had two kids in college, another living in their house and a bunch of medical bills coming due. Ellen and the chair person agreed that I should go.

Sitting in a meeting with several other pastors, one of them asked "how's your dad?" I informed them he wasn't doing very well and I was going to see him the next week. "How long will you be gone?"

"Four days." I said.

"Are you looking forward to spending some quality time with your dad?" They didn't know the story.

I said, "I think so….I'm not really sure….This will be the longest I have ever spent with him alone in my life." They looked stunned. I'm sure I did as well. It had not occurred to me until that moment. To my knowledge, I had never spent four days with my dad. Weird.

I spoke with Ellen, she set out to pray me through it. She was beginning to understand how big of a deal this had been for me in my life. Her upbringing was classically good. She knew both her parents well, knew they loved her and while every family has its "junk" she had never really understood how much my relationship with my dad had affected me. Not because she didn't want to know, rather because I nursed my own wounds, kept my grudges to myself and only let her see the darkness in me that I was willing for her to see.

With some trepidation and an uncomfortable feeling of ignorance, having no idea how to do this or how it would go, I arrived at the airport in Tampa. I was picked up by the father of my step-mother (who, by the way, is only nine or ten years my senior) and we headed east. I arrived at my dad's house in a suburb of Tampa mid afternoon. I saw my dad - almost bald, no teeth, thin, cancer grey, lying in bed with a tube coming out of his stomach. "Hey bud," he said.

"You look like crap," was my response. It was exactly what he expected and wanted from me, this much I knew…honesty and humor. The next four days, to be frank, were pretty boring. He slept most of the time. It was February and I lived in Michigan, so I went running each day and sat in his room most of the time otherwise. He watched Fox News and ESPN. I don't mean he turned them on now and then, I mean one of them was on 24/7. I don't watch sports, and an hour or two of news is more than my limit in a day. I would love to say we had an absolutely wonderful time together. I would be thrilled to tell you we finally had that time I had asked for on the golf course a decade and a half prior…a fantasy father/son time. We were just together. We talked, he slept. I helped him get to the shower and back to his bed, he slept some more. I got to know his wife a bit and I fixed all three of their computers and set up a new wireless printer and upgraded their wireless network. In other words, it was exactly what it should have been. When dads come to visit, they fix things and help out around the house. When sons visit their invalid (albeit temporary in this case) dads they fix things and help out around the house. It was normal.

## *~ The Circle Closes ~*

My last full day in Florida, while driving my dad to his radiation treatment, he began to talk about his life a bit. Like most people who have had to look the reaper in the face, coming to grips with their own mortality, my dad was taking inventory. He began to tell me how he had been given a second chance; a second chance to make his life something worthwhile. He told me he didn't want to waste it and wanted to make right the wrongs he had done. Driving his aging Lincoln in an unfamiliar city, I made a choice. Instead of listening and trying to figure out a way to subtly remind him of all his wrongs, instead of fishing to find out if the wrongs I was considering were the same wrongs he was regretting, instead of trying to make this conversation about me and my needs, I decided to be his pastor. Thinking of my brothers and their kids, of my wife and my kids, I listened and when he asked, I gave him the following advice, "I encourage you to try. Take it slow. But keep in mind your kids are adults now. They don't need the daddy who left, they have other needs now. They have kids, jobs, spouses. And they may not feel the need to re-establish the relationship the same way you do. Make yourself available to them and respond with grace if they are not initially receptive. They will learn your motives over time. They just might not trust them yet."

******

*It worries me a bit, as I write these pages. I fear the reader may think I am trying to show how 'good' I am. Remember, please, this conversation is thirty years in the making. If I were good, this new found attitude would have taken hold twenty-seven years ago. I am a stubborn man with a strong sense of justice. Over three decades I moved from being hurt and wounded, to being vengeful and hateful, from being forgiven to forgiving, and back to begrudging and stewing, from not caring to pitying, and finally from compassion to honesty. Honesty with myself about who I allowed myself to become, and honesty about my dad - who he is, as well as who he will likely never be.*

******

I went back to Michigan, home to my wife, kids and church. Was I changed? Yes. Did anyone notice? I don't think so. The difference was in my soul. It had been wounded, time and time again, but it was healing. When parishioners asked about my dad, "How's he doing, still cancer free?," I would genuinely smile and say in the words of my dad, "Yup, still cancer free and on the right side of the dirt."

All these years he had been living rent free in my head and I desperately wanted him to pay the back-rent he owed. As it turns out, he had moved out years ago, I never bothered to check the dwelling. It would have been nice to have another tenant living there, keeping the place clean and looking lived in. Better late than never.

# *Chapter 10*
# *"Clichés"*

I am a believer in a statement learned while working for Young Life during college: "You have to earn the right to be heard." This arises from 1 Thessalonians 2:8 and was taught to each volunteer as a philosophy of ministry to disinterested high school kids. Just as Jesus became one of us so that we would know how much He loves us, that He understands from experience what it means to be human, we are to share our lives with others, going where they go, to live where they live before we have any right to speak into their lives. The right to be heard must be earned by the speaker and given by the hearer. I'm hoping at this point that I've earned the right to be heard by you. I have shared with you most of the journey with my father who is now my dad. I have tried to pull back the curtain and let you see how my mind works and what my struggles are. While this is a monologue and I am unable to hear your story or live where you live, I hope you will grant me the opportunity to speak (or teach) and that you will 'hear' the truth in the words, paragraphs and chapters that follow.

***1 Thes. 2:8 (NIV)***

> "We loved you so much that we were delighted to share with you not only the gospel of God but our lives as well, because you had become so dear to us."

As I consider trying to teach in the chapters that follow, I think it appropriate to dispel or correct some clichés people have tried to use to "encourage" me over the years. Notice "encourage" is in quotations. To encourage is to inspire with courage, spirit or confidence, to impute strength and to stimulate right thinking and action. These statements did not accomplish that.

## *~ "Time heals all wounds" ~*

What a load of hooey! I have heard this cliché offered, spouted and espoused dozens, if not hundreds, of times. People offer it to women whose husbands have cheated on them, to men rejected at work, to friends who have suffered loss, even to children whose parents split up. Time does not heal all wounds. In fact, I am not sure time heals any wounds; maybe nicks and cuts, scrapes and muscle pulls, headaches and hangnails, but not wounds.

As an example: When I was twenty three years old, I was in a van heading from Chicago to Tallahassee, FL to work on a Habitat for Humanity house. Just past Rensselaer, IN on I-65 the driver of the van lost control and flipped the van. I was sitting in the front passenger seat. As the van rolled over, I put my right hand on the ceiling to brace myself. As the windows burst, much of the glass found its way into my right forearm. I will spare you the details. The injury I sustained and the journey that followed has enough for a book all by itself. Suffice it to say, the glass severed two nerves and the major artery in the lower part of my arm.

What would time do for that wound? Actually, the more time that passed the closer I came to dying. Time would not heal that wound, intervention was needed, a transfusion was necessary and surgery would be required. Then, if all went well, it would take time before I would know if healing would be complete or partial.

Time does not heal wounds. It saddens me when I meet Christians who believe time will heal wounds to the soul. Maybe it's true in some cases; distance from the harm, sin, victimization, loss or hurt will ease the pain enough that one can move past it, but that has never been my experience. When my soul is wounded, when someone considers his needs or desires over mine, the only thing that helps me get through it is surgery on the soul. I have to open things up, take a look around, clean out the infectious material, suture what is torn, close the wound and then put the salve of the Holy Spirit on the surgically altered wound. Initially, this means more pain, not less. This means the cost is born by me, not by the person who did me harm. It is tiring, difficult and painful. However, the result is this: a healing wound, though limiting in some ways, is not a wound that can be infected. I will know my limitations because I have seen the injury for what it was. There will be scar tissue but no festering microbe or infectious pathogen waiting to do me more harm in the future.

As stated earlier, in my experience forgiveness is not something accomplished in a one-time prayer. In fact, I do not think forgiveness is something that can be accomplished at all. It must be lived. It's not something I do, it's something I practice or train for. I will never be at a place where I have forgotten my wounds. I can choose, however, to live in such a way that I am no longer crippled by them.

## ~ *"Love means never having to say you're sorry"*~

I believe this cliché came into fashion after the movie, "Love Story," was released in 1970. I have never seen the film, nor am I sure what the plot was. However, my experience with this sound bite has been both painful and freeing.

I agree with the saying to some extent. In premarital counseling, I advise couples *not* to say they are sorry, but to ask for and give forgiveness. While this is not the way the cliché is meant to be used, it does work well in relationships. The cliché has come to mean this: you don't have to apologize to those you love and who love you because if you are truly loved, those who love you will accept you wholly and therefore will accept your flaws, misdeeds, brash words and insensitiveness. I could not disagree more.

If this were true; if I am never obligated to express sorrow for the wound I caused another person, then I would never be helped by others in my growth toward becoming the man God wants me to be.

The fact is, God commands us to confess our sins to one another (James 5:16). Jesus says in Matthew 18:15 (NIV), "If your brother sins against you, go and show him his fault, just between the two of you. If he listens to you, you have won your brother over." In Luke 17:3 (NIV), "...If your brother sins, rebuke him, and if he repents, forgive him." It seems to me, if we were not expected to express sorrow (say "I'm sorry"), Jesus would not have encouraged the wounded party to approach the one inflicting the wound.

With that said, there is an idea that remains in our culture. Often, when I say "I'm sorry," what I mean is this: "I don't want to talk about this anymore." When the wronged person says, "That's OK," there is an unwritten understanding. "That's OK" means this: "I'll let you off the hook this time, but the next time you do something that resembles this I reserve the right to recall this event." The end result of this mutual understanding is score keeping. Nothing is ever brought up for the last time. Wrongs are remembered (which is understandable), but because the wrong was never settled, grace was never given and mercy never received, the right to rehash wrongs done remains in the hands of the one who received the wound.

If I hurt you, wrong you or am insensitive toward your needs, wants, desires or person, I should be called to give account. My motives may have been pure, my desire may have been altruistic, and my actions may have even been necessary, but if I wronged you, we should deal with it, not ignore it. Personally, I do not believe people are capable of ignoring wounds. I remember just about every time someone has wronged me. I also know some of the wounds I have inflicted (unintentionally) on my wife, daughter and son. In fact, this book may inflict a wound on my dad, though that is not the intent. If we try to ignore wounds, they fester.

I do not advocate apology because seldom have I been satisfied with an apology offered to me. And whenever I apologize to someone I have wounded, I still feel in his debt. On the other hand, I do recommend we practice forgiveness. If I wrong Ellen and become aware of that wrong, I should approach her and confess –tell her what she already knows – and ask for her forgiveness. When I ask for forgiveness I am not asking for her to forget, rather I am asking her to give me what I do not deserve…Grace. When I ask, something changes in me. I no longer have to be right. My opinions do not need to be heard and my motives do not need to be acknowledged. When she gives forgiveness, whatever the wound was, whatever wrong I did her has been brought up for the last time. The ability to keep score has been given away. Think about it for a second. If you are in a relationship of any kind and you are keeping score of wrongs done and effort given, who is winning? You are, right? If I asked the person you are in relationship with what would he/she say? He's winning, right? When I keep score, I win, but *we* lose. I did this for years with my father and until I quit he was never going to be my dad.

If you bump into someone in the kitchen, say "I'm sorry." Anything more serious than that, ask for forgiveness. Love means never having to say you're sorry but it also means you promise to ask for and offer forgiveness.

## *~ "I have a right to be happy" ~*

I am born, bred and raised as an American. I am as patriotic and appreciative of the freedoms we have as any Christian ought to be. With that said, I am going to state something that does not sound very American. I do not have the RIGHT to be happy. In fact, I have no rights at all except those God gives to me. The Declaration of Independence of the United States of America says, *"We hold these Truths to be self-evident, that all Men are created equal, that they are endowed by their Creator with certain inalienable Rights that among these are Life, Liberty and the pursuit of Happiness."* Notice the phrase "and the pursuit of Happiness." Even in our founding documents, we are not told we have the inalienable right to be happy, but to pursue it. But here's the rub: if I pursue happiness it will likely remain just beyond my grasp. For example: When I was in middle school, I couldn't wait to be in high school. I thought my social issues would be solved, freedom would be given and life would have more joy. Once in high school, I still had to ride my bike, bum a ride or walk wherever I wanted to go. I couldn't wait to get my driver's license. Then I wanted my own car, then college, a job, money, wife, house, more money, family, more money, etc. There is always something else required before I will be 'happy.' If happiness were a right and the pursuit of happiness guaranteed happy experiences, we would be the happiest, most optimistic culture ever to exist. Bad things wouldn't happen, politicians would tell us the truth and not what we want to hear, and God would be thrilled with our stewardship of the planet, our finances and our care for the poor.

I would argue that pursuing happiness will leave us ever wanting. However, if I concentrate my behavior toward doing what is good, right, noble, excellent, admirable, praiseworthy and altruistic, if I am concerned for you before being concerned for me (Philippians 2:3-4), happiness may very well be the byproduct. In other words, if I pursue happiness I will likely never be happy. If I pursue faithfulness I will likely be happier. If you think about it, this is the reasoning behind volunteerism; doing that which costs you (time, energy and effort) for the benefit of others. What is the result of giving yourself for the benefit of other people? Contentment, joy, satisfaction, pride and …yes…happiness.

Let's put these ideas in context. Our subject? Forgiveness. Jesus says the following:

**John 14:15 (NIV)**

"If you love me, you will obey what I command."

**John 14:23-24 (NIV)**

"[23]Jesus replied, "If anyone loves me, he will obey my teaching. My Father will love him, and we will come to him and make our home with him. [24]He who does not love me will not obey my teaching. These words you hear are not my own; they belong to the Father who sent me."

**John 15:10-14 (NIV)**

"[10]If you obey my commands, you will remain in my love, just as I have obeyed my Father's commands and remain in his love. [11]I have told you this so that my joy may be in you and that your joy may be complete. [12]My command is this: Love each other as I have loved you.

> [13]Greater love has no one than this, that he lay down his life for his friends. [14]You are my friends if you do what I command."

If I love Christ, I will obey Him. If I obey Him I remain in His love. His desire is that His joy will be in me and my joy will be complete. What does he command me to do? Love others. How? By doing what He did, laying myself down for others. That includes my rights. It includes my right to hold a grudge, to lick my wounds and the right to be right. So how do I love someone who has wounded me, hurt me, taken advantage of me or treated my like chattel? By how I behave, not by how I feel. Paul – author of 2/3 of the New Testament - says to the church in Corinth:

**1 Cor. 13:4-7 (NIV)**

> "Love is patient, love is kind. It does not envy, it does not boast, it is not proud. [5]It is not rude, it is not self-seeking, it is not easily angered, it keeps no record of wrongs. [6]Love does not delight in evil but rejoices with the truth. [7]It always protects, always trusts, always hopes, always perseveres."

Take a look with me at this description of love. Which of these phrases or descriptors is about "me"? Only one....love is not self-seeking. Which is about how I *feel*? Only one....not easily angered. The rest, and even the two highlighted immediately above, are about how I am to behave, not how I am to feel. If Jesus' command is to love others, and love is defined by how I behave selflessly toward others....keeping no record of wrongs...then forgiveness of wrongs is the goal, not happiness. If Jesus' command was given so that His joy would be in me and my joy would be complete, then it stands to reason; as I love and forgive, His joy will be in me and my joy will be growing in completeness.

All this is to say God wants us to have joy in our lives. He wants to give it to us. We cannot be happy without His joy. We cannot pursue happiness and attain it. And you and I will never be truly happy as long as we 'keep records of wrongs."

I am called to first be a citizen of heaven, a child of God, an heir to the throne of Christ. All this is before I am called to be an American ever in pursuit of happiness. It stands to reason that God knows what will make me happy better than I do. Most of my life proves that point. Hatred, bitterness and reveling in my wounds only produced fruit that was rotten and harmful. My hope…my prayer is that you will give up your rights to justice for the wrongs done to you, hoping happiness will be yours when justice is served. It won't. Happiness only comes from love, love comes from behavior, and keeping record of wrongs is not part of loving behavior. I know this is hard, but it is right.

God will call those who have wronged me to give account. Likewise, He will call me to give account for not doing what is right….forgive.

## ~ *"Forgiving is forgetting"* ~

This cliché is nothing but dung. Even God says He remembers our sins no more. He doesn't forget, He decides not to remember. You've read about my view on this previously. This is just a reminder. I do not believe I will ever forget either the wounds inflicted upon me or the wounds I have inflicted on others. However, while I will not forget, I can hold them loosely in open hands, trusting God will be both just and merciful as He deals with them. While I will remember, I will not be controlled by them. I will likely not forget, but I will not imprison myself because someone else was once in my debt.

Forgiveness, between two people, is not absolution. It is an acknowledgement that harm was done, and a choice to behave in such a way that love wins, not rights.

# *Chapter 11*
# *"Undeserved Power"*

## *~ On One Condition ~*

After offering forgiveness to my father and replacing the vows made as a child with vows made as a young man, replacing vengeful vows with vows of mercy, I began to study, learn and preach more passionately about this journey, this great work of God, this healer of wounds, this spiritual practice. Forgiveness became a teacher I wanted to learn from continually. These are the lessons I learned.

The only conditional thing in all of Christianity is forgiveness. This is not a conclusion I came to on my own, it is a conclusion Jesus states very clearly on more than one occasion. God loves me no matter what. There is nothing I can do to keep God from caring for me, just as there is nothing either of my children can do to keep me from caring for them. Likewise there is also nothing I can do to save myself from sin. I am wholly incapable of being so good that God has to accept me. I am saved by grace (getting what I do not deserve). It is not because I have any merit before the Lord, but because He has chosen to love me…to love me even though. There are no conditions to God's love for me. As a believer, a follower of Christ, I am an heir to the Kingdom and promises of God…period. His love is there, I need only receive it….accept it. Once I have done that, there are some expectations placed on me. I am to forgive as I have been forgiven.

Remember the parable of the unmerciful servant from chapter five? The servant was forgiven much but would not forgive little. What happened to him? He ended up in prison until he could repay his own insurmountable debt. Jesus speaks to this idea elsewhere. Look at Matthew 6:14-15 (NIV) where Jesus says, "[14]For if you forgive men when they sin against you, your heavenly Father will also forgive you. [15]But if you do not forgive men their sins, your Father will not forgive your sins." In Matthew, the disciples (Jesus' closest followers) asked Jesus to teach them how to pray. He recited what is now known as the Lord's Prayer, in which he says, "forgive us our sins as we forgive those who sin against us." He immediately followed that prayer with the verses you see above.

If I forgive men when they sin against me, I will be forgiven. If I don't….I won't. Ouch. This "if…then" statement seems harsh. What if I can't forgive? Why would He put that on me? I thought He loved me no matter what and that my sins were forgiven when He died on the cross. God is God, forgiving is something He has to do. If I forgive the person who hurt me, aren't I saying what he/she did is OK?

I have resonated with the objections of many people who have shared with me their struggles: How can I forgive my father when he doesn't acknowledge the pain he caused? How can I forgive the young man who killed my son in a car accident? If I forgive him, it means that what he did didn't matter...that my son didn't matter. If I forgive my father for abusing me, I'm letting him off the hook.....he was my father, there's no way he should be off the hook! How could God ask me, *command* me to forgive this person? If any of those questions are even close to what goes on in your mind, please read on. I have some ideas.

## ~ *Undeserved Power* ~

As you have read, my father lived rent free in my head for many years. As is true in all real estate transactions, the value is determined by the market and the market is determined by location, location, location. My father was living in prime real estate and I was paying his rent for him. He didn't know how often I thought of my wounds. He didn't know how I resented him. He may have had a clue now and then, but he was concerned about his life, not mine, just as I was concerned about my life, not his. My father didn't know how much my psyche, personality, motivations, hopes, dreams, ailments and struggles stemmed from what he did and what he didn't do. My father didn't know and (at the time of writing this) probably still doesn't.

As I surgically probed my wounds, I found the source of pain. My father was concerned about himself instead of being concerned about my mother, my brothers and me. He wanted to be happy, didn't think he was happy in his marriage with my mom and believed he could be happier with someone else....someone other than my mother, someone other than me. This is what hurt. And when I think about other people who have sinned against me or wounded me, I come to the same conclusion: when people hurt me, they are considering their desires, wants or needs over mine. I become a consequence, a bystander, an intended or unintended casualty. It hurt because I (or someone I love) was treated with disregard, no better than old furniture to be left by the side of the road, or like a toy to be played with and then thrown away. In other words, my wounds have come from someone exerting power over me they did not deserve to have. Powerful people are powerful because they have authority or means to control others. They are able to make decisions, call shots and control outcomes that either benefit themselves at the expense of others or benefit others at the expense of themselves. When my father exerted power in my life, he was making decisions that benefitted him at my expense. *I* paid for *his* happiness. *His* 'happiness' cost *me*. I wasn't consulted, asked or given the chance to speak. I paid a tax without representation. He exerted power over me and I didn't like it.

I resented him for years because he chose himself over me. He demanded 'payment' from me for his pleasure. I was angry because he had the power to hurt me and chose to wield it. As my father, he had authority to teach me, mold me, even make me into the man I was supposed to be, and he didn't. Instead, he taught me I was not worth his time or effort. I was worth less to him than was his own happiness. He molded me, unbeknownst to him, into a bitter young man who took years to get past being the abandoned little boy. He made me think I was lacking as a son, as a man and even as a pastor. I honestly believe he didn't know these things, but these were the fruits of his authority and power over me. Or, at least the fruit of the power over me that I gave to him.

Here's the kicker. When he made his decision to leave, he harmed me by choosing himself over others, exercising power he did not deserve over the rest of the family, and taking control over how my life would go from that point forward. He took power over me that he did not deserve. But sixteen years later, as I was resenting him, was embittered toward him, and even hating him, I realized I was *giving* him power over me that he did not deserve. Ironically, he didn't even know he had it. I let him control my feelings. I let him make me angry. I allowed him to control how I saw myself. I (in a way) even asked him to confirm the view I had of myself by watching for actions and decisions that agreed with my assessment of him and his motives. He had hurt me initially because he was selfish. He continued to hurt me because I let him. In fact, I wanted him to. I WANTED him to. Really. I know that sounds sick, but I did. I wanted him to be the jerk I thought he was. I hoped he would continue to think he had done a good job 'raising his boys' even though he was absent. I relished in the opportunities to tell others of my pain because it would make me look that much better, stronger and more faithful. When he left, he sinned against me. After he left, the sin was mine. I gave this man power over me that rightfully belongs only to God. I kept my father from being my dad because I wanted him to know he wasn't my dad. I hoped he would realize what he was missing. I wanted him to pay, but instead the bill continued to come to me.

He never knew the power he had over me. He may have known that his leaving was difficult on the family. He may have asked God to forgive him for his selfish choice. But he never knew how powerful he was. And this saddens me. Not because he didn't know how much I suffered but because so much of my life, so much of my identity, was dictated by the undeserved power I gave him in my life. So much of who I could have been and what I could have done was poisoned by this single event in my life. It was as if I spent years drinking poison hoping it would make HIM sick. I know this is ridiculous but it is what happens when anyone chooses not to forgive - poisoning self, hoping it will make the one who hurt us sick. It doesn't. It won't....ever.

So why does Jesus instruct us to forgive people when they sin against us? Why does He put conditions on it: "For if you forgive men when they sin against you, your heavenly Father will also forgive you. [15]But if you do not forgive men their sins, your Father will not forgive your sins."? Because He loves us and wants what is best for us. Because He knows that our unwillingness to forgive others when they harm us will put US in prison to be tortured. It will poison US. Because He understands that if we hold on to the sins committed against us we are trying to make a bet we cannot cover. We are, like the unfaithful servant, demanding payment for a debt owed us from someone who has no ability to pay. He knows we are demanding rent from the perpetrator but are paying it ourselves. Jesus commands us to forgive so that we can be forgiven AND so we can be free.

## *~ A gift that should never have to be given ~*

Friends of mine have suffered a horrible tragedy. Four years ago their oldest son was killed by another young man who had been drinking one night and decided to drive home. I don't know the specifics of the events or the sentence the young driver received, but I do know some of the fruit of these experiences, and it's rotten. I pray to God that I never have to bury one of my children, but if I do, I pray it is not due to a reckless, needless accident like this one. I can only imagine how I would feel the day I heard the news or the day the young man was sentenced. I do know, however, how I would likely deal with the next years.

I would want the young man to grow old in prison. One time mistake or not, if he took the life of my son, he should 'lose' his life. I would nurture my pain as an offering to the lost life of my son. I would never forget and likely never forgive. If the perpetrator had ended the life of my son, I would want his life to be over.

My wife knows friends of the other family…the family of the young man who messed up and drove home drunk. She knows the other side as well. The anguish, hurt and pain of watching your son go to prison, knowing he made a mistake that ended the life of another kid. She's prayed for the family of the one who took the life of the son of our friends. She knows their pain, heartache and the lifelong price of this mistake. She has seen the fruit of this, and it, too, is rotten. I pray to God I never have to watch one of my children make a mistake like this one. I can only imagine how I would feel the day I heard the news or the day my child was sentenced.

There was nothing good that came from this tragedy. One kid's life ended. The others' did too, though differently. This was a no-win scenario. Understandably, forgiving the young man who killed our friends' son seemed impossible. It would be like saying "my son's life didn't really matter." Forgiving the driver would be saying, "My son is forgotten. So I MUST be angry so I NEVER forget."

While I do not understand how this feels, I do understand the motive. I know the father of this lost son. He struggles each time we offer communion at church. "How can I receive 'grace' from God when I cannot forgive this kid who killed my son?" As his pastor, I've tried to explain. I've tried to help him see. And he tries, he hears and he sees. He is beginning a life long journey of practicing forgiveness. What he is coming to realize is that forgiving this young man who killed his son is not equivalent to saying "what you did was OK (or right)." Forgiveness from one person to another is not absolution; it is taking power away from the wrong-doer, power that does not belong to him. Deciding to stay angry long term is like walking into a prison cell, closing the door behind you, swallowing the key, and saying to the wrong-doer, "You're never getting out!" While he may deserve to be in the prison, locking yourself in a cell does not punish him; it punishes you. Deciding to let oneself out of the cell is not the same as saying "killing my son doesn't matter" or "it's OK, don't worry about it." It simply acknowledges that he no longer has the power to make you miserable. He did wrong and had the power to kill your son, but he does not have the power to imprison you, unless you do it to yourself and blame him.

# ~ *Idolatry?* ~

When I don't forgive, I am demanding rent for the real estate in my head and on my soul. Jesus commands me to forgive that debt so that He can pay it in our stead. Ellen, my wife, had a revelation a few years back. I do not remember the context or how the insight came about, but she shared this with me one day. She said, "I'm beginning to understand that if the blood of Jesus is sufficient to cover or forgive my sins, it is also sufficient to cover and forgive the sins others commit against me."

Wow. You would think that a pastor would have known this sooner, seen and understood this truth. Seminary, it seems, should have been very clear on this matter. I don't know if it is my individualized faith that kept this from me or simply my 'stuff' with my dad. If my sins are forgiven by Christ, others' sins are too; even those committed against me. If Jesus' death is good enough for God, shouldn't it be good enough for me? If God has forgiven a sin (or all sins) committed against me but I refuse to do the same, aren't I exerting power over another that Christ Himself has chosen not to exert? Aren't I demanding payment from the perpetrator of harm done to me while God has already paid the debt?

This gets tricky. John 20:22-23 says, "[22]And with that he breathed on them and said, "Receive the Holy Spirit. [23]If you forgive anyone his sins, they are forgiven; if you do not forgive them, they are not forgiven." To His disciples, Jesus gives authority to forgive sins. If I am a follower of Christ then I am His disciple. If I forgive anyone his sins, they are forgiven. I can live with that. However, it's the next line that troubles me. If I do NOT forgive another, they are not forgiven. How do I reconcile that with the command in Matthew that I must forgive in order to be forgiven? Theologians will debate between individual responsibility (Matthew 6) and the authority of the church as it pertains to the apostolic ministry (John 20) but either way, I do not want that kind of power.

Please keep in mind, these are conclusions I have come to in my own head, heart and life. None of this is intended to foster guilt. Quite the contrary; my hope is you will find freedom in forgiving as you have found freedom in being forgiven.

Since Jesus' sacrifice is sufficient to forgive my sins and is sufficient to forgive the sins of others, even those who have sinned against me, if I choose not to forgive, to hold a grudge, to ever be mindful of the wrong done to me, aren't I exerting power over another that I do not deserve? In effect, I am claiming to be a god over another. I am judging him for the wrong he has done, even though The Judge has decided to be merciful. If I choose to harbor a grudge, hold a debt or punish a trespass against me, I am, in a way, making myself an idol; exerting power in another's life that rightfully belongs only to God.

# *Chapter 12*

# *"Figures of Speech (Metaphors and Similes)"*

Throughout this story I have used several word pictures, analogies, metaphors and similes. Some have kind of come to me in the process of writing, others I intended to use from the day I decided to put these things to paper. In this final chapter, I want to clarify, expand, articulate and teach.

## *~ Living Rent Free in My Head ~*

I don't remember where I heard this metaphor but I know I have only heard it once. About two weeks before I began the sabbatical my church graciously offered me, during which I would be writing this book, I found a scrap of paper with these words written on it: "Rent Free in My Head. Use in book." I remembered writing it but don't remember when.

I've found the figure of speech to be both colloquial and profound. It communicates so much with so few words. Song writers do this. What would take a romance novelist three hundred pages to convey, a lyricist can communicate in three and a half minutes.

My dad, whom I dearly love, lived in my head rent free for almost thirty years. At least that's how I saw it. As I reflect on my story and growth, I realize he was never actually living in the prime Real Estate I had given him. His name was on the mail box but the bills came to me. I am saddened to say I don't think I ever took the time to go into this penthouse apartment to confirm it was actually being lived in. It was furnished. The electricity was on. Gas bills increased as the whether became cold. I often heard noises up there and wondered why he was being so loud, but honestly, I don't think my dad ever lived there. It was a phantom, a ghost, a spirit I locked away in this dwelling to remind me of my fears, wounds and uncertainties.

I truly hope it is clear I am using another metaphor. I don't actually hear noises and haven't really paid any bills. There is no actual entity living in an imaginary penthouse in my head. I simply want to show how much all of this cost me. I grieve the joy I lost from all the years of paying his rent in my head, especially now that I realize he may have had this apartment but he never even knew it existed.

Please, if there is someone living rent free in your head. If someone has wounded you and as a result still controls how you think, what you think, who you are or what you do, go check the penthouse. If you are honest with yourself and see what is really there, you will most likely find you are paying rent and bills for no one. It is costing you dearly and the one who hurt you doesn't even know the apartment exists.

Forgiveness cancels the lease, evicts the 'tenant' and frees up all the resources you have been paying in monthly bills, insurance fees and collection agencies.

## *~ Sophomore / wise-fool ~*

This word comes from two Greek words combined to make one. Sophos is Greek for wise. From this word we get the name *Sophia,* which means wisdom and the adjective *sophisticated* which means altered by education and/or experience so as not to be naïve. Moros is Greek for foolish or dull. From moros we get English words like *moron* and *morose*. This term was likely picked for a second year student in high school and college because a student in such a time in life is likely one who has begun the refinement process but is still dull or naïve.

I chose this word carefully because I am a sophomore. While I have a high school diploma, a Bachelor of Arts degree and a Masters of Divinity degree, I am as foolish as I am wise. I am ever becoming more sophisticated but often like a moron.

As I have worked on this book I have been disgusted with myself for taking so long to learn this simple truth: God forgives so we can forgive. I have always known I should forgive and have learned over the years that forgiveness costs me, but coming to grips with the heart of God and understanding that He has forgiven me so that I CAN forgive others, not just so I WOULD forgive others, is proving to be beyond my ability to truly grasp. Imagine a world where there was no mercy, where we always received what we deserved, a world with no grace, where we never received what we didn't deserve. There would be no joy, no laughter, no surprise and no hope for something better. God wants His joy to be in us and our joy to be complete. If you are holding a grudge, living in unforgiveness, waiting for acknowledgement of your pain before you offer mercy, I have one question for you, "how is that working out for you?" Just like the invalid in John 5 who would never receive from the pool that which he needed, so it is with you, with me, with us. We will never experience that which God has for us if we don't buy into a new system.

Consider this. In the passage mentioned above, when Jesus said to the man who had been an invalid for thirty eight years "Get up!" What would have happened to the man if he had continued to tell Jesus why he couldn't get up? Jesus is God in flesh. When God speaks, things happen. When Jesus said, "Get up!" the invalid was healed. Done. Finished. Over. But what if the man never obeyed the command to get up? Would he have ever experienced the healing? If he just lay there, would he ever walk? No. He had to respond to the command of Christ in order to experience what was already done.

We are commanded to forgive and because of Christ we CAN forgive. We can allow the blood shed for our sins to be sufficient for the sins committed against us. It may not happen overnight. But we must respond to the command. When the invalid stood up, my guess is that he was wobbly. He probably tired easily and had to re-learn how to participate in society as an able bodied man. But he could *walk* when previously he couldn't. So it is with us. We CAN forgive so we can walk....move on....move forward.

Forgiving is wise but it is hard. Fools do the easy thing and fall into folly; the wise do what is difficult because it is right. I am both wise and foolish. But as far as forgiveness is concerned I seek to become more *sophos* than *moros*.

## ~ *War – truce, forgiveness* ~

There is a war in the universe and there is a war in your mind. The battles are different but the prize is the same. God has an enemy who is fighting to own you, control you and destroy you. Battles take place in the heavens and few have been witness to these tactics or weapons. But battles take place, too, in the minds of men. We are each familiar with the tactics and weapons in this arena.

Picture it like this. In you there lives both a wolf and a dove. The wolf is a predator, slinking and stalking around, stealthily looking for what it might devour. The dove coos, flies and roosts. The wolf represents sin, evil and hatred; the dove love, joy, peace, grace and mercy. If these two animals are continually battling in your mind, which one is going to win? The one you feed. If you feed one, you starve the other. The wolf's appetite is voracious. It makes a lot of noise, growls, howls and barks. Because it is loud and its nature is to prey on weaker creatures, it demands your attention all the time, it needs flesh. The dove needs only grain and seed, sits quietly cooing, waiting for whatever you will toss it. It doesn't demand much and flies away when the wolf comes to feed.

If these two are at war in you, which one do you want to feed? The one seeking to steal, kill and destroy, or the one that has come to give life and life in its fullness? Feed the dove. There will never be a truce between the wolf and the dove. They will never peacefully coexist. One must starve for the other to thrive.

During a talk show on the radio the other day I heard a commentator say, "There is not peace unless there is victory. The victor sets the terms for peace and the defeated accepts the terms without prejudice." I agree....at least as it pertains to the war for our hearts. There is no peace unless there is victory. Christ is victorious and has set the terms for peace, "forgive as the Lord has forgiven you."

Forgiveness is surrender to Christ and His terms for peace. If I choose to continue to fight for justice and acknowledgement for wrongs done to me, I will not win. I can't. The enemy isn't even fighting. By not forgiving, I'm firing mortars and smart bombs on my own property. It doesn't harm the perpetrator of wrong, it feeds the wolf living in me.....and it starves the dove.

## *~ For-giving not for-getting ~*

One of my dear friends has been reading this book as I write it. She has edited, commented, and let me know when things are working and when they aren't. The day she sent chapter three back to me she commented on one of my faith lessons. I thought I was being clever but she told me it didn't work. The play on words went like this: "forgiveness is for giving, not for getting." Seriously....I really thought this might end up being one of those things other people quote and attribute to me. I was very impressed with myself. However, upon further reflection I decided to change the verbiage and explain it more fully at the end of the book.

There is a reason the infinitive form of the verb "to forgive" has at its root "give." When practiced, forgiveness is a gift. It is something which costs the one forgiving and is received by the recipient at no cost. Typically we give gifts to those we love or like very much, though sometimes we are obligated to purchase an item to give to another for whom we have little affection. Regardless of the motive, gift giving costs the giver not the recipient.

Forgiveness is hard. It is an act of the will. It is an ongoing offering to God and a gift that continues to cost the giver. Forgiveness is for giving. There are those who have counseled me, and will likely counsel you, that forgiveness means you forget the wrong done to you. I could not disagree more. I cannot forget the wounds I have received. I wince each time they come to mind. Internally I know I waited and waited and waited for my dad to give me some indication that he regretted the things he had done. And as I received bits and pieces of his regret, I found they didn't satisfy my longing. Finally, I came to the conclusion that they never would. In order for me to forgive my dad, I had to come to grips with the fact that I would not 'get' anything in return from him. Forgiveness is for giving, not for getting.

As I grew, learned and taught on the topic, I came to realize what I consider a great truth. Throughout scripture people are corrected for giving to God in practice but not giving to God from the heart…with pure motive. I found myself going through the motions of forgiveness but never being wholly honest about the cost. I discovered that God did not desire platitudes and ritual but a continual act of my will. I learned I had to be willing to continually live, "not my will but Yours."

In 1 Chronicles 21, King David was commanded by God to build an altar at the site where an angel had appeared. David went to Araunah the Jebusite, the owner of the spot, and asked to purchase the site at "full price" so that he could build an altar to the Lord. Araunah was reluctant…not to sell, but to take payment. He even offered to give items for offerings to the Lord. David replied (in summary), "I will not give to the Lord that which cost me nothing."

God is not honored in my life when I offer pseudo or partial forgiveness any more than I would be satisfied if God forgave some of my sins. Forgiveness is a gift given to another who has done me harm. It costs me dearly. I will not give to the Lord that which costs me nothing. Not all sacrifices are offerings but all offerings demand some sacrifice. I choose, daily, to offer to God that which costs me dearly. I forgive my dad.

## *~ Background Music ~*

Several years ago while preaching a Christmas Eve sermon, I suddenly lost all the hearing in one of my ears and much in my other. I was able to finish the sermon, but when I awoke the next day I still couldn't hear with one ear and barely in the other. As it turned out I had contracted a virus that severely damaged my ears. To this day there are sounds I cannot hear. My family and friends often laugh at my misunderstandings. Certain letters (f, s, c, t, th, etc) are indistinguishable to me. Therefore, if I cannot see the speaker's mouth, my brain fills in the blanks. Often what I 'get' is far from what was said.

This is a mild inconvenience but it often changes how I interpret things. For example: the other day I was watching a television program. There was a patient on screen who "coded." There were no visual clues to the emergency, only a 'flat line,' high pitched tone that I could not hear. The medical team began to run about, readying the 'crash cart' and injecting things into the patient. Meanwhile, I had to ask my wife what was going on. I had no clue I had not received the audible cue I had been given to help me interpret the scene.

I have learned to cope and my family has learned to fill me in when I look at them…confused. I have come to appreciate how non-visual cues help interpret a scene. Similarly, wrong or comedic non-visual cues can give a whole different meaning to a scene. Years ago, there was a British sketch-comedy skit where comedians were shown a scene from an old movie. There was no sound, so the comics were given microphones and asked to ad lib what was going on. Their intent was to misinterpret the scene, thus eliciting a humorous response from the audience.

Over the years I have come to realize that I have had the wrong background music playing when interacting with and interpreting the actions of my dad. In Psychological circles this is known as expectational bias. One tends to interpret events, motives and actions in a way that one expects the person to behave. Allowing my expectation to interpret the motive of my dad has been like letting the score of a movie create an atmosphere of foreboding before the frightening event takes place. It is subtle but very effective. My problem has been that I have played the wrong soundtrack, the wrong score in my head as I watched events unfold. This is stinkin' thinkin' and I resolve to turn the volume down from now on and take the cues from the scene itself. I pray you will do the same.

## *~ Drinking Poison ~*

Unforgiveness or 'carrying a grudge' is like drinking poison while hoping the one who did you harm will get sick. If I have earned the right to speak into your life at all, please learn this lesson, heed this advise and find freedom. The comedian Buddy Hackett is quoted saying, "...I never carry a grudge. You know why? While you're carrying a grudge, they're out dancing."

The net affect of carrying a grudge is a burden you carry, poison you drink and joy you lose. It does not impact the one who injured you nearly as much as it impacts you. Siblings lose years of familial interaction. Sons lose moms and dads they long for. Fathers and Mothers lose children they love. Friends lose shared experiences and support. Why? Pain that is never given the chance to heal.

Granted, we are never commanded to be stupid. If you have been sexually assaulted, abused and/or controlled by another person. If you have been the victim of a sociopath, a habitual criminal or if you have been betrayed and deceived by another who has a history of such behavior, you are not expected to be the victimizer's friend. You do not need to trust the untrustworthy or place your children in the care of a child molester. God does not expect or want us to be foolish...quite the contrary. However, we are expected to return evil with kindness, bless those who persecute us and pray for our enemies. Notice the scriptures make no bones about the fact that we do have enemies, evil is done to us and there are those who just want to do us harm. When you forgive someone who has done evil things to you, you are not absolving them of wrong; you are simply deciding not to allow them to continue to have power over you that they do not deserve.

God will deal with evil. He will punish horrific acts. Let Him right the wrongs – those done to you by others. Offer Him your right for revenge and for acknowledgement of your pain. Allow Him to compose the background music in your mind. Give Him the rent free space in your head. Let God be God so you don't have to be, and stop drinking the poison that only hurts you.

## ~ *Already/Not Yet* ~

Every year before Christmas many Christian churches celebrate the season of advent. Advent is a time in the church year that feels to many a bit pretentious. We 'pretend' to anticipate the coming of Christ even though we know He has already come. There is a second reason for advent – looking forward to Christ's return. The Messiah has already come but He has not yet returned. The Reign of Christ has begun but it is not yet fully realized. God has kept His promises but there are promises not yet fulfilled. God has already won the war but we have not yet experienced His enduring promise of no more tears.

I have already forgiven my dad but I have not yet fully lived that forgiveness in my life. My sins have been paid for but I am not yet without sinful behavior and thoughts. My hope is you will join me on the journey to rid yourself of undeserved power in your life. It begins today but the journey is not yet complete. In your life there may be a prodigal father, an undependable friend, an accidental perpetrator of harm or a sociopathic abusive relative. No matter who has done you wrong, you have suffered enough. Jesus says, "The thief comes only to steal, kill and destroy; I have come that you may have life and have it to the full" (John 10:10 NIV). The enemy's desire is to steal your hope, kill your joy and destroy your faith. Often, he uses people to accomplish his desires, but they only have the power to accomplish that which the enemy intends if you give it to them.

## ~ *Freedom* ~

I began this chapter in mid June 2009. After finishing a page or two I put the computer away and traveled with my family for a while. The day we returned, my dad came to the area for a visit. He was staying with one of my brothers and for seven days there were barbeques to be had, ball games to attend, wake boarding and fishing to be done and politics to be discussed. Claire was busy, Scott had friends to hang out with and I didn't particularly want to make the forty minute drive to my brother's house every day, but we did what families do – we put other stuff on hold to be family.

During that week, only once did I get a twinge from the background music. Only once did I get the bitter taste of poison in my mouth. Only once did I have the thought that 'rent was due.' My dad asked, "How's the writing going?" For a moment I felt guilty. For another I felt angry. Five seconds later I realized he just wanted to know how my writing was going. He is a dad asking how his son is doing with his first attempt at writing a book. What should a father ask? I answered, "It's going well. I hope one day my kids will read it and know my story and my 'junk.'" He smiled and said, "I'm sure they will."

I watched him with new eyes that week. I was free to see him for who he is. He swelled with pride at Claire's mission work and desire to pursue ministry as a career. He loved to see Scott's effortless athletic ability. He rejoiced watching Trip and I pull the six youngest children tubing behind Trip's ski boat. He spoke well of my mother, bragged on his sons and even took the grief we gave him when he kept talking about his recent surgery. It was as it should be.

Three days after he returned to his home I received a voicemail on my mobile phone. He thanked me for the week and said, "It was one of…nope…THE best week of my life."

While I am certain there are other reasons for his joy, I know in part, he was blessed because I am free. I no longer have to pretend I want to be around him. I'm sure he didn't feel like he had to earn the right to be grandpa and dad. For the first time in his life, at least as far as my efforts are concerned, my dad felt like I let him be my dad. That may not be how he would put it, but I know it was something new. The debt has been paid, the poison cleansed and the prison door has been left open.

## ~ *My prayer* ~

Lord, re-write the score in my head. Accept my offering of pain and resentment as one given you freely of my will. Redeem the years lost to carrying a grudge. Forgive me for taking so long to learn this simple truth and forgive my dad for leaving me. Give my children a greater measure of wisdom than you have given me so they will not suffer the consequences of undeserved power in their lives. Finally Lord, I pray my children forgive me for however I have wounded them.

I know how powerful a father's words and actions can be. May I never live 'rent free' in either of their heads.

In the Name of Your Son, Jesus I pray.

Let it be so.